LILLIAN WALD

LILLIAN WALD

LILLIAN WALD

The Nurse in Blue

BY SALLY ROGOW

Paintings by Itzhak Sankowsky

The Jewish Publication Society of America
5726-1966   *Philadelphia*

First printing 1966
Copyright © 1966 by The Jewish Publication Society
of America
All rights reserved
Library of Congress Catalog Card Number: 66-11719
Manufactured in the United States of America
Designed by Richard Palmer

Introduction

As a young graduate nurse, Lillian Wald came to New York's lower East Side to "live as a neighbor" to the thousands of immigrants streaming into the "Golden Land," America. Among their numbers were Lithuanians, Roumanians, Hungarians, Irish, Germans and Jews. The Jews, like the others, were fleeing from poverty, and also from the pogroms of Eastern Europe.

Amidst indescribable poverty, suffering and squalor, Lillian Wald, a child of wealth and comfort, battled the whiplash of epidemic diseases, smallpox, typhoid fever, diphtheria, and tuberculosis.

The Visiting Nurses Association began as an idea in the mind of this pioneering young nurse, and it eventually grew into a beacon for public health nursing around the world.

Lillian Wald also forged the first link in a "chain of

friendship" that today circles the world with the work of the World Health Organization, the International Red Cross, and the city and county agencies across the length and breadth of America.

This courageous woman's battle with the appalling suffering that was "everywhere to be seen" brought her face to face with the social conditions of poverty. From public health nurse to pioneer social worker, Lillian Wald became one of the giants of the twentieth century, taking her place beside such humanitarians as Jane Addams, Jacob Riis, Herbert Lehman, and Stephen Wise.

Founder of the Henry Street Settlement House in New York, Lillian Wald became a leader in the abolition of child labor, champion of the Federal Children's Bureau, advocate of international cooperation for the promotion of world health, and spokesman for world peace.

Lillian Wald was not afraid to hold a dream, nor was she content with dreaming. A woman of action, Lillian Wald aspired to fashion reality out of the fabric of her ideals.

"And God's eternal truth lies folded deep in all man's lofty dreams" (Ann Preston).

Contents

LILLIAN WALD

1. *A Shattered Dream*

The fire glowed in the brick fireplace; its flames crackled and sent great shadows dancing about the room. There was a time when Lillian would have invented a story about the filmy, graceful shadow dancers and told it to her brother Alfred. But not now, not today . . . and the way she was feeling, not ever.

Lillian battled with the turmoil of feelings inside her. First she was angry, then lonely, miserable—and then angry all over again. She crumpled the letter in her hand and tossed it into the fire.

"I hate him. He doesn't care one bit about me," Lillian whispered furiously to herself. "No, I don't hate him," she decided on second thought, "but he is foolish. He's going to turn into a silly playboy." Lillian finally gave in to her misery. She threw herself on the deep blue plush chair and began to sob.

Her sobs brought her mother rushing into the parlor. "What's wrong, whatever can be so terribly wrong?" Minnie Wald asked, seating herself next to Lillian. "Tell me," she said softly, stroking the thick black curls away from Lillian's brow.

"It's Alfred. I'm so unhappy now that he has decided to stay in California." Lillian wept more softly. Alfred, her older brother, her dearest friend, Alfred, who had always understood her, had let her down.

Alfred had been sent to California to take care of Uncle Samuel's business. He liked it so much that he wanted to stay. As far back as Lillian could remember, she and Alfred had planned their futures together. They had a great plan: Alfred was going to go to Medical College and become a doctor, and Lillian was to be his assistant. Alfred was more than just a part of Lillian's future. He WAS her future. How all this was going to work out, Lillian did not know. But at fifteen, she did not have to know. As long as Alfred was near, Lillian did not doubt that a great and glorious future lay ahead.

All that was gone now. Alfred was in California, and he planned to stay. He didn't want to study medicine, or anything else. And Lillian was no longer a part of his plans.

Minnie Wald looked at her daughter. It was hard to believe that a girl could miss her brother so much. She had known how close Lillian and Alfred, her two middle children, were, but she could not know how much Lillian had counted on her brother.

"Remember," Minnie said, trying to comfort Lillian,

"that Alfred is happy. He is doing what he wants to do, and he is doing it very well."

"But he was supposed to be a doctor," Lillian muttered angrily.

Suddenly, she sat up and looked hard at her mother. "If Alfred won't go to college, then I'll go," she shouted.

"My dear, you are being impulsive. Why should you even want to go to college? Young ladies do not need to go," Minnie answered in a soft voice.

"Why should being a girl make any difference at all? I'm a person, too. You were going to send Alfred, so why shouldn't you send me?" Lillian was very excited now.

"You are only fifteen now. You'll change your mind. You are a very privileged young lady, and a wonderful life is waiting for you," said Minnie soothingly.

"I don't want that kind of a wonderful life. I want to do something important, something that matters. I don't want to spend my life at society teas," Lillian almost shouted at her mother.

Minnie Wald looked hurt. Lillian had never shouted like that before. Minnie had never raised her voice to her children. "You have a party to get ready for, so please, dear, run along and get dressed," she said quietly.

"You are taking me too lightly. I was never more serious," her daughter said in a lower tone of voice. She did not want to hurt her mother, but she felt that she had never wanted anything as badly as she now wanted to go to college.

Disturbed by the noise, Lillian's older sister, Julia, came rushing into the room.

"What's all this fuss about? Lillian, you are being very

rude to Mother, shouting at her like that. I heard you all the way upstairs."

Lillian's face turned very red. Julia could say things that cut her to the quick. Life was so very simple for her tall attractive sister, and she could not understand the more complicated Lillian.

"You are a silly fool to be making such a fuss. Soon you'll be a debutante, and if you don't "come out," you'll miss the most fun of a girl's life."

"I don't care. I am going to college, and nothing can change my mind," Lillian answered her sister.

"Lillian dear, listen to me," pleaded Minnie Wald, who had never seen her daughter so upset. "Men do not like women to be intellectual." Mrs. Wald had her heart set on "good" marriages for her daughters. Lillian's outburst was deeply disturbing to the fashionable matron, who could not visualize a life for Lillian that was any different from the one that she herself had lived.

Max Wald was a highly successful Rochester businessman, and he had given his family every comfort and luxury they could have wanted. He was an indulgent father, and could deny nothing to his beloved children. When Lillian had gone to her father for help, Max had listened quietly to Lillian's argument, and then had said, "Let her go to college, if that's what she wants."

"Thank you, thank you." Lillian had hugged her father and flown up to her room to write a letter to the President of Vassar College.

After the letter went off, Lillian waited for the postman to bring a reply. She did not doubt for a moment that she would be accepted into the college, for after all, her marks had been excellent. She had been a good student at Miss Cruttendon's School for Girls.

When the long white envelope bearing the reply finally came, Lillian quickly tore it open. Her face, which had glowed with anticipation just a few seconds before, now was shadowed with disappointment. The President of Vassar had been sympathetic . . . but he had advised Lillian to apply again when she was older. A very subdued Lillian returned to Miss Cruttendon's School.

The girls at Miss Cruttendon's were all from very privileged homes. Along with French Literature, Mathematics, History, Geography and languages, the girls were prepared for life as members of the leisure class. Parties and teas were so numerous that it seemed as if they were part of the curriculum.

Minnie Wald enjoyed the parties more than Lillian did. Both Julia and Lillian had good figures, and she loved to fuss over their clothes. Julia loved the elaborate gowns and the endless fussing of her mother over her appearance, but Lillian had no patience for the tedious fittings.

"Stand still please, Miss Wald," pleaded the dressmaker, "otherwise I'll never be able to fit your gown properly. And please, put down your book." The dressmaker sighed. It was always such a chore to fit the younger Miss Wald. Lillian shifted from one foot to the other, rustling the sapphire blue taffeta.

Lillian was a good student, and she was popular with the other girls at Miss Cruttendon's. Her poems and stories were highly praised by her teachers, who always almost instantly warmed to the eager, bright-eyed and vivacious girl.

Life in the Wald household was gay. No one seemed to suspect the driving restlessness that haunted Lillian's thoughts. And Lillian herself could not have put her feelings into words. Perhaps it was just part of growing up. But again and again, Lillian's thoughts dwelled on Alfred.

She missed him more and more as time went on. He had been too good a companion, and Lillian had never felt the need for other friends.

When Lillian was eleven and Alfred thirteen, they had organized their own theater, with the elder Walds and little Gus, the youngest brother, as their steady and appreciative audience. The big livingroom, with its deep comfortable chairs, its cherry-red damask drapes, its rich jewel-colored Oriental carpets, was often the setting for their lively performances. Sometimes the other children of the neighborhood were invited to an elaborate production in the open air theater of the Wald garden.

Closest in age of the four Wald children, Lillian and Alfred were also closest in interests. When the family had lived in Dayton, Ohio, Grandpa Favey, Mrs. Wald's father, had built a little house for the children to use as a dollhouse. Inside there was real furniture, and a stove that they could actually use for cooking. The dollhouse had been the scene of many hours of play. Alfred pretended to be a great surgeon, and with Lillian as his nurse, they saved one doll after another from the ravages of disease.

Lillian's grandparents on both her mother's and fa-

8

ther's side had come to America from Germany, where both families had had wealth and influence. The failure of the Revolution of 1848 had brought them to America in search of nourishment for their democratic ideals. As with many of the newcomers to America of that time, they had a vigorous faith in the new country, along with refinements and ideas from an age-old culture. A love for music, poetry and literature was as much a part of the Wald household as its silver service and snow-white linens.

Lillian and Alfred fed their imaginations on Grandpa Favey's wonderful tales of the old world. The operas, the plays, and the story-book dollhouse stimulated their sense of drama and adventure.

Perhaps Alfred could still be persuaded to come home. Perhaps it was not too late. Lillian wrote Alfred a long letter, pleading with him to come back.

But Alfred never received Lillian's letter. The very day after it was written, the Walds received news that cast a long black shadow over the household: Alfred had drowned.

Hope was gone now. It gave way to a terrible grief. Minnie Wald became sick with heartache; weak and ill, she could not summon the strength to leave her bed. Lillian's gentle father carried his sorrow in silence, like a burden on his back. He seemed to have grown old with its weight.

Life, which had been so full of love and comfort, now seemed empty to Lillian. A light had gone from the Wald household, and the family never wholly recovered from the shock of Alfred's death.

Lillian experienced a new kind of loneliness. She could not even think of college now. Her mother was unhappy enough, and Lillian could not think of adding another hurt.

Without Alfred would Lillian ever experience the excitement and freedom of the world outside of Rochester society?

In an effort to cheer her mother and spare her the fear that her daughter was "different," Lillian prepared herself to be a gay debutante. But the round of parties did nothing to quiet the restlessness that persisted inside of her.

Lillian was graduated from Miss Cruttendon's School with honors. But shortly afterwards she complained to her father: "I'm so bored. Please find me something to do."

It was unthinkable for a girl in Rochester "society" to look for a job. In fact, there were no jobs for women in the business world in the 1880's. A woman's place was in the home. But Max Wald understood his daughter, and he found her a job as a correspondent for the Bradstreet Company. It was a job she could do at home.

Lillian did the work well, but stocks, bonds and mortgages were too dull for a girl who yearned to venture into the world outside where important things happened.

The warm golden sun of summer awakened Lillian's desire to travel. She went to visit her sister Julia, who had a summer house at the seashore. Julia was married now; she was Mrs. Charles Barry, the wife of a young and successful Rochester businessman.

Lillian relaxed at Julia's summer house. The salty spray of the sea refreshed her. However, during one of the many pleasant afternoons that the two sisters spent together sitting on the beach, Julia complained of feeling dizzy, and her face became very pale. Lillian brought her back to the house and put her to bed, made her comfortable, and put a cold cloth over her eyes before she went to telephone the doctor.

"Miss Wald, you have a real knack for nursing," said the doctor, who noticed the care Lillian had given Julia. "But your sister needs the care of a professional nurse," he added.

Lillian was hurt; she was sure she could have taken good care of Julia all by herself.

"He said I had done well," she told herself. But Lillian did as she was instructed and went to get the nurse whose address the doctor had given her.

Almost as soon as the door was opened and the friendly nurse appeared, Lillian knew she had found a friend. After the nurse was established in Julia's home, Lillian bombarded her with questions and listened avidly to the nurse's description of her life at Bellevue Hospital in New York. The nurse explained to Lillian the difficulties of establishing nursing as a profession. Lillian began to want to be a part of it.

While Julia was recuperating under the nurse's care, Lillian was mending a broken dream.

The wheels of her mind were turning at a faster and faster pace. Nursing would get her out into the world. Nursing would mean a different way of life. Nursing was important. Yes, nursing was the answer and nursing it would be. Lillian felt a new excitement quicken her pulse.

Despite the heroism of Florence Nightingale and Clara Barton in establishing nursing as a profession, it was still thought of as an "unwomanly" occupation in the 1880's. In Rochester "society," a nurse was little more than a house worker. The very word "nurse" had undignified associations.

"It's a new profession and nurses are very badly needed," Lillian told her mother as she launched a tidal-wave campaign to crush parental objections.

Minnie Wald was her old self again. She had never fully recaptured her old zest, but she was active once more.

"No Lillian, you can't consider it. Why, what would everyone say? The gossip does not disturb me nearly as much as what would become of you." Mrs. Wald saw all her ambitions for her pretty daughter going up in smoke. Mr. Wald wasn't much help to his wife; he always gave in to his children. Besides, no one knew better than Minnie how useless it was to oppose the willful Lillian.

Lillian applied to the New York Hospital in New York City for nurses' training, and the hospital requested that she come to New York for an interview. Her brother-in-law, Charles Barry, agreed to accompany her.

"You will see," Charles said to his mother-in-law, "how quickly Lillian will give up her notions once she is inside the hospital."

Miss Sutliffe, Director of Nurses at the New York

Hospital, looked at the well-dressed young woman who stood before her. She liked the direct way Lillian had of looking at her. But Miss Sutliffe had had plenty of experience with high-minded girls, who dramatically saw themselves as angels in white. When it came to the test, these girls could not make it: they had been fooling themselves.

But this one, with the glossy black curls and the steady eyes, she just might succeed. The Director went against her better judgment, and followed the intuition that told her that Lillian had the courage and persistence to follow through. "Miss Wald, I have accepted your application," she said.

"Thank you, thank you," Lillian almost sang out for joy.

In September, 1887, Lillian Wald entered New York Hospital as a nurse in training.

2. In Training

It was late in the afternoon, and Lillian was walking down the basement corridor of the hospital when she heard sobbing and shrieking. At first she did not know where the sounds were coming from, but as she approached the padded cells the shrieks became louder.

The only thing Lillian could think of was the terrible suffering behind those terrible screams. She had to open the cell and help whoever was in there. Student nurses were not given the keys to the cells, but Lillian remembered that the elevator man had a set of keys.

The elevator man hesitated to give his keys to a student, but Lillian was persistent and the man relented and gave her the keys.

When Lillian finally opened the door of the cell, she

found a disheveled old man weeping and holding his stomach as if he were in agonizing pain.

Lillian entered the cell and the man looked at her with glazed eyes. "I am being starved," he cried. "I'm so hungry. They don't give me anything to eat," he moaned.

"Be patient a little while longer," Lillian said sympathetically, "and I'll go and bring you back a nice tray of food."

In a hurry to get food for the old man, Lillian did not even lock the door of the cell. She remembered that student nurses were not supposed to be in the kitchen, but no rule was going to keep her from helping an old man half-crazed with hunger. Lillian snatched a tray and piled it with dishes that she found in the hospital ice box.

"Hospitals are supposed to help people, not to punish them." Lillian felt her temper rise at the way the old man appeared to have been treated. How grateful he had been when she had brought him the food.

The next day, Miss Sutliffe asked Lillian to come to her office.

Lillian felt her cheeks burning, and she tried to avoid Miss Sutliffe's eyes. But the keen Director of Nurses kept her glance steady. She was determined that Lillian learn the importance of a hospital rule.

"I understand the sympathy you felt for the patient, but a hospital must have rules or nothing would ever get done," Miss Sutliffe said firmly. "You took food that was specially prepared for one patient and gave it to another, on impulse. A nurse must use her head as well as her heart."

Lillian could not think of anything to say. Of course Miss Sutliffe was right. But the old man was so hungry; how could she have refused to bring him a meal?

"Do you know why the man was in a padded cell?" asked Miss Sutliffe. "You were a brave but very foolish girl to open that door."

"Why?" Lillian managed to ask.

"The padded cells are where we keep the alcoholics. They are designed to protect themselves and others from them until they can be safely put into the wards. Food was offered to that patient at every mealtime, but he refused to take it. Alcoholics usually do not care to eat until the effects of the alcohol have worn off. The patient would have been properly taken care of at the evening meal."

"Oh," Lillian murmured—"I am truly sorry Miss Sutliffe. I guess I'm too headstrong."

Lillian couldn't wait to leave the Director's office. Her face was smarting with the confusion of feelings inside her.

"One more thing, Nurse Wald," Miss Sutliffe smiled. "I probably would have done the same thing myself. That poor old man was probably crazy with hunger."

Resentment and shame melted away in an instant. Miss Sutliffe really did understand, and Lillian felt reassured. Perhaps she was not a failure as a nurse, if only she could keep from defying the rules.

Hospital regulations were strict, and Lillian bristled under the discipline they imposed. The student nurses were supervised by Miss Sutliffe and only one other graduate nurse. The nursing staff was made up mostly of the student nurses, who had to learn by performing. They scrubbed the wide corridors, fed, bathed and medicated the patients. All the work had to be done according to a strict schedule.

Lillian Wald entered New York Hospital at the very beginning of serious education for nurses. Miss Irene Sutliffe was one of the pioneers in a field that had been in the dark ages until the Civil War. Florence Nightingale had proven the value of competent nursing, but the idea of a training school for nurses was barely accepted. Professional nurses were in the middle of their battle for recognition of their profession.

Miss Sutliffe believed that if the student nurses themselves were unaware of the discipline of their profession, the outside world would never learn to appreciate the need for the careful training of nurses.

Miss Sutliffe trained her students without the assistance of textbooks or teachers. If she did not impose rules and regulations, she would never be able to instill discipline and respect for hospital routine in her nurses.

Lillian tried hard to do what was expected of her, but it was impossible for her to treat the patients in her care in an impersonal way. Everyone had a story to tell and Lillian enjoyed listening. She joked and laughed with the patients, and time seemed to fly away. She could be seen rushing about the wards, hurriedly making the beds. Sometimes she was even late in bringing meals, all because she had spent too much time in one of the wards or with the children.

After a while, Lillian did learn to channel her energies where they would do the most good, and she appreciated the value of a firm administration. While she never became a slave to the rules, she learned to respect them.

For a young woman whose every whim had been indulged in childhood, this was no simple achievement.

Lillian managed to pass the period of probation without incident, and the day arrived when she was given the uniform of the student nurse.

Standing before the large mirror, Lillian could barely hold back the laughter that was bubbling inside her. She had to admire the image in the mirror.

The new uniform was a blue plaid dress covered by a long white apron. The little white cap sat upon Lillian's mass of black curls like a proud bird in a nest. Student Nurse Wald was no longer on trial.

Nurse Wald had one more obstacle to overcome before she could consider herself a full-fledged nurse, and that was her fear of the operating room.

Lillian gathered up her wide skirt and tucked it under her knees. She scrubbed the floor with vigorous strokes.

"Hospital floors should be as clean as can be," she told herself, scooping up the soapy water from the pail. Though she would not admit it, she was aware that her devotion to scrubbing floors was partly a ruse designed to keep her out of the Operating Room.

"Nurse Wald," said Miss Sutliffe, walking out into the corridor, "a patient of yours, Miss Finnegan, is about to be wheeled upstairs. She is very nervous. I'm sure she would be much more comfortable if you were to accompany her."

Lillian felt her heart pound under her starchy uniform. She put away the pail and scrubbrush and dried her hands, rubbing them as hard as she could as if she could rub the nervousness out. She put a smile on her face before she went in to Miss Finnegan.

The small gray-haired woman reached for the nurse's hand. "Oh Nurse Wald, I'm so glad that you are here," she said.

"Of course I am here and I'm going to stay with you, too," Lillian's voice was low and soothing and she held Miss Finnegan's hand in a firm grasp.

"I won't die, will I?" Miss Finnegan put her final fear into words. And Lillian thought, "Here am I, frightened only by my own feelings, while Miss Finnegan is the one who's going to be operated on." Lillian tossed her head, as if to shake off her own fears. And suddenly she felt the warm glow of a new strength, the kind that comes from thinking of the feelings of other people.

"Miss Finnegan," said Lillian with a wide smile, "soon you are going to feel like dancing. Get those silly thoughts out of your head. You are going to get well, I promise you."

"I feel better already," said the little bird-like woman, who held tight to Lillian's hand all the way to the Operating Room.

In the Operating Room, Lillian was kept so busy getting things ready and keeping instruments sterile, that she had no time to think of being afraid.

"It wasn't nearly as bad as I thought it would be," Lillian glowed with relief. It had been a private victory, and Lillian felt very much the "nurse" as she left the Operating Room.

With a cheery jangle of keys, scissors, pins and

thermometer case hanging from her waist, Lillian tended the patients in Ward G. She made a special point of knowing the names of all the patients in her ward, many of whom had no families, no homes, no money.

"How all alone a person must feel when no one even bothers to learn his name," she thought, and resolved never to forget a name.

Lillian was naturally friendly, and she took a personal interest in each one of her patients. They soon came to trust her: here was someone who listened to their troubles and never made them feel ashamed.

"Surely, it is no crime for a man to have an illness too costly to pay for," Lillian reassured the patients, whose pride made them ashamed to be on charity. In no time, Lillian had become the most popular nurse on Ward G.

Lillian graduated from the New York Hospital in March, 1891. "You have become an excellent nurse, Lillian, and I personally would like you to stay on here and join the staff," Miss Sutliffe said to Lillian on the day of graduation. Lillian wanted to hug the small, stern woman. She had never worked with anyone whom she admired as much as she did Miss Sutliffe.

"Oh, Miss Sutliffe, I couldn't be more pleased," said Lillian smiling. And then she added, "and honored." And so she joined the small staff of trained nurses.

"Hurry home. Your father is very ill," read the telegram that shook in Lillian's trembling hand. But when she arrived in Rochester, her father had already passed away. "I wasn't even here," she cried brokenheartedly.

Filled with guilt and remorse, she decided to stay at home.

The big house was too empty, too full of memories of that gentle man, who could deny nothing to his family. Lillian and her mother lived alone in the old family home. Julia had her own home and Lillian's younger brother, Gus, was in business outside of Rochester.

"It's so strange here now, with everyone gone," Lillian confided to her mother.

"I know," said Minnie Wald. "And it's too hard on us. I want to move in with Julia, Lillian. You are too young and have too much spirit to be content for long staying in this big old empty house with me. And besides, I can be useful at Julia's house, with my grandchildren."

And that was how it was decided. Minnie Wald moved her belongings into Julia's house, and Lillian returned to New York.

Lillian found out that the New York Juvenile Asylum needed a nurse. "That would be wonderful," she thought. "I always wanted to work with children." She was full of hope during the long trip out to the Asylum.

The grounds were lovely. The Asylum was set in twenty acres of oak grove. Lillian did not learn until later that the children were not allowed outside the high stone wall that fenced in the Asylum itself on only four acres of land.

The New York Juvenile Asylum—a cluster of grimy buildings—was home for the "truant, disobedient, friendless and neglected" children of New York City.

"All that beautiful grove going to waste," Lillian sighed to herself when she discovered that the children were only allowed outside of the wall to work in the fields. "It's just made for children to play in."

Lillian often stood at the window of the tiny room that served as her office and watched the children hard at work outside. "All the children do here is work. They farm, they clean, they cook. And in the time left over, they sit in the dingy schoolrooms. There is no time for play, the very thing that children need the most." Lillian felt very sorry for the small people hard at work right under her window.

There were too many children . . . and too few adults to supervise them. The only way that inevitable mischief was to be avoided was to keep the children busy.

And as if that were not bad enough, boys whose only crime was that they were orphaned and had no one to care for them were thrown together with young delinquents. The orphans were treated the same as the delinquents, and imprisoned as if they had committed a crime. Too often, the innocents came to admire the hardened delinquents, and they, too, became experts in the ways of the underworld.

"I didn't steal. I swear I didn't." Lillian heard the frightened sobs from her office.

"What's wrong, I wonder," thought Lillian, getting up from her desk to investigate.

In the matron's office, the matron was standing over a boy with a leather strap in her hand.

"Please, please don't hit me," nine-year-old Timothy was pleading. "I swear, I swear, I didn't steal."

"That's enough swearing," said the matron, about to

lower the strap. Then she saw Lillian standing at her door.

"What is the matter here?" asked Lillian, shocked at the matron's cruelty.

"Timothy is a thief and I'm going to punish him. I'll give him something to remember in case he ever wants to steal again," said the matron, hardly looking at Lillian.

"Tell me the truth, Timothy. Look at me and tell me, did you steal?" Timothy looked at the nurse. "No mam, I never. . . ." He couldn't finish, and the tears ran from his eyes.

"I think I believe you, Timothy," said Lillian.

"He stole once, Nurse, and he was caught." The matron was annoyed at Lillian's interference.

"How can you expect a child to be good, if you don't have any faith in him? Timothy should at least have a trial," Lillian argued.

Timothy was given a trial, and after all the evidence was heard, he was declared innocent. But for Lillian this was too small a victory in a hopeless battle. Timothy was only one boy. There was too little help for too many children. She felt helpless and hopeless, in the midst of a medieval institution where children were treated with coldness and distrust. Her hands were tied, she could not reform a reformatory. At least not while she was employed there as a nurse.

An idea began to grow on Lillian. "If I went further into medicine and learned more, I could do more." Nursing was confined to institutions. And institutions are rules and regulations. Lillian wanted to be on her own, among people, "where I can do something that matters."

Perhaps if I had more training, there would be more opportunities," she thought. Lillian enrolled at the Women's Medical College of the New York Infirmary.

Medical School was a challenge, and Lillian worked hard at her studies. But the papers and books and lectures could not shake the old restlessness from her spirit. She yearned "to do." But "do" what, that she did not know.

Mrs. Loeb, a wealthy philanthropist, decided to finance a class for young immigrant women, to teach them the basic principles of home hygiene and first aid. Lillian was asked to teach the course at an old school on Henry Street.

Lillian jumped at the chance. "At least I'll be doing something worthwhile," she said enthusiastically.

3. A Way to Serve

The class in Home Nursing at the old technical school on Henry Street was almost over. The women shifted restlessly in their seats—and Lillian felt that she was making no impression. "At least I can show them how to make a bed," she thought, pulling a sheet from her bag.

The white sheet billowed and then lay flat. Lillian pulled it taut and was tucking the corners underneath a small mattress, when a little girl came sobbing into the room.

"Nurse, please come," the girl cried, running to Lillian.

"What's wrong?" Lillian asked the trembling child, who began to tug at her sleeve.

"It's my mother: she is sick, awful, awful sick. Come with me," the girl managed to plead between sobs.

"Of course I'll come. We'll go right now." Lillian pulled the sheet off the bed and stuffed it into her bag.

She hurried after the girl, nearly tripping over the slippery refuse scattered on the sidewalk. Icy pin drops of the cold March rain stung her eyes; and the overpowering stench of garbage filled her nose. Street after street, the odors changed and grew worse. At the end of Ludlow Street, there were barrels of rotting fish lined up on the sidewalk. Lillian held her breath. The unbearable stench that rose from the barrels permeated the air.

Lillian followed the girl. They went into a rickety tenement at the rear of a narrow alley, and climbed a flight of grimy steps, muddied with years of footprints, then out through a dark alley into an open court. It was a nightmare of mazes and alleys, and Lillian wondered where she was being taken.

Finally, the girl pushed open a door, and Lillian entered a small dark room. On a crumpled bed, stained with blood and grime, lay the girl's mother. Her face was chalk-white and tense with pain. Next to her sat her husband, a lame beggar whose face was lined with sorrow.

Lillian examined the woman and washed away the crusted blood and grime from her wasted body. The clean sheet soon replaced the bloodied rags and covered the rotting mattress that served as a bed. After Lillian had made the mother as comfortable as she could, she turned to the baby.

The family of seven was sharing their two bleak tiny rooms with boarders. Lillian went out and brought food back for the entire family. The children stared with

wonder at the food that was cooking on the small gas burner. Lillian wondered when they had last eaten, so quickly did the food disappear from their plates.

Scrubbing the floor with the strongest solution she could stand, Lillian managed to noticeably brighten up the rear tenement.

"God bless you," said the woman, pressing her lips to Lillian's hand.

When Lillian left the tenement, her hands smarted from the strong solution and her back ached with fatigue, but she felt a strange exhilaration as she walked along the darkening streets. The sights and sounds of the East Side filled her ears and jumbled her thoughts. She was haunted by the memory of that woman's face.

Yes, there was work for her here. The plan seemed to come to her in a flash; its simple logic dispelled her confusion. Lillian knew that she wanted to live on the East Side, be a part of its life and share its burdens. Walking faster now, Lillian couldn't wait to tell her friend, Mary Brewster, a fellow nurse, of her plan. If only Mary would agree to live on the East Side with her.

Lillian had known only the comfort and safety of a large home. Yet there was something on the East Side that seemed to attract her. Perhaps it was the miraculous fact that the people survived here, that they raised families and never completely gave up hoping. The women in the Home Nursing Class, the mother she had just visited, all of them were trying to make better lives for their families. They had not given up.

"How could such suffering exist?" she asked herself over and over again. "Was the city outside unaware of conditions on the East Side?" Lillian had been ignorant, perhaps others were too. But she was sure that once people were told, and saw for themselves, then surely, prosperous citizens would do something. "Now that I know, I'm going to tell, I'm going to see to it that others know too," Lillian thought to herself, confident that the wealthy and influential would want to help.

Lillian and Mary Brewster talked late into the night. Mary was infected by Lillian's enthusiasm, and she agreed to the plan. Slim and delicate featured, the blonde-haired Mary was as different from Lillian as night from day. But they were a team now.

The very next day, Lillian visited Mrs. Loeb, the generous woman who had financed the class in Home Nursing.

Lillian spoke quickly. Her cheeks were flushed and her eyes sparkled with excitement as she explained her plan to Mrs. Loeb. "You can see how much good two nurses will be able to do."

"My dear child," said Mrs. Loeb gently, "I wonder if you realize the size of the job you are undertaking. Have you any idea what living on the East Side will be like?"

"I'd like at least to be able to find out. If we cannot do anything, we will be the first to admit it, Mrs. Loeb." Lillian looked directly into the eyes of the older woman: "Please give us a chance to try."

"I can hardly refuse in the face of such determination." Mrs. Loeb smiled at the intent expression on Lillian's face. Privately, she thought that a few days of living on the East Side would cure the young nurse of her enthusiasm.

Mrs. Loeb spoke to her son-in-law, the financier Jacob Schiff, and they each agreed to give sixty dollars each month for the support of the two nurses. Lillian dropped her studies at the medical school.

Lillian and Mary combed the East Side for a suitable apartment. "My only demand is that the apartment have indoor plumbing," said Lillian. "I'm spoiled, but I refuse to live without a private bath."

Apartments with indoor plumbing were very scarce on the East Side, but the search led the nurses to the College Settlement on Rivington Street.

The College Settlement was housed in an old brick house that had once been a mansion. Graceful stone columns adorned the front of the house. Lillian admired the elegant old door as she rang the bell.

Lillian introduced herself to the young woman who answered the door. Dr. Jane Robbins and Miss Jean Fine, fired by the same spirit that now moved Lillian, welcomed her to the College Settlement.

At lunch, Jean Fine described the plan of the Settlement House to Lillian. "Nurses would be a God-send in this neighborhood," she told Lillian. "You and your friend can certainly live here with us until you find your own place." Lillian was overjoyed. The nurses moved into the Settlement that very afternoon.

Dr. Jane Robbins and her co-workers at the University Settlement had been inspired by the work done in Whitechapel, London, where Toynbee Hall, the first Settlement House in the world, was opened in 1884. In the good company of these pioneer social workers, Lillian became acquainted with the problems of the neighborhood. She soon discovered that the problem was much more than to "know and to tell."

At the College Settlement, Lillian met Jacob Riis, a devoted reformer and writer, and learned of the work of Jane Addams, founder of Hull House in Chicago.

From early morning until late at night, Rivington Street bustled with the sounds of pushcart merchants hawking their wares; the shouts of pots, pans, clothing and food merchants mingled with the sound of children at play. Yiddish, German, Italian and English blended together in the life of the street. The smell of overripe fruit, hot bread, and sweaty clothes permeated the noisy and bustling street.

Lillian felt very much at home on Rivington Street. The sights and sounds of the lively street life were exciting. People were friendly here. Lillian enjoyed the informality and closeness of the community.

Jacob Schiff advised Lillian to get approval from the Board of Health before she went into people's homes as a nurse. Lillian made an appointment with the President of the Board of Health. The President was reluctant to give his permission to such a venture at first. He did not want to take responsibility for two unknown nurses.

"We certainly will be of no bother to you. And besides, we could keep records and submit them to you for your own use," Lillian pleaded. "And," she went on, "we could be helpful in other ways. You know that Mr. Schiff suggested that I come to you."

"It would be helpful to have more statistics than we

now have," the President said in agreement. Lillian's mention of Jacob Schiff's name had worked like a charm. The President also agreed that the nurses should wear a badge reading, VISITING NURSE, UNDER THE AUSPICES OF THE BOARD OF HEALTH. Lillian laughed at her own audacity. She had pulled rank on the President of the Board of Health and it had worked.

In May, 1893, Lillian and Mary Brewster pinned their badges on their blue uniforms and went to work.

Lillian was worried lest people mistake them for nurses sent out by one of the religious charities. "I would not want 'Visiting Nurses' to be considered a charity," Lillian explained to Jacob Schiff. "People must feel free to call on us. And they won't if they think our services are free."

Only the very desperately ill called upon the various religious charities for nursing care. Many preferred to suffer rather than let their neighbors know that they were forced to accept charity.

"The badge will help," Lillian thought, "but we also ought to charge a very small fee. Even if people can only pay a dime, it will help them to think that they are paying for their care."

"And if they can't pay, we simply won't charge. Or we can let them owe us the money," added Mary.

Lillian wanted people to be able to call on them directly. She wanted them to know that the services of "Visiting Nurses" were immediately available, and did not have to wait upon a doctor's referral.

The nurses that were sent out by the charities only answered a doctor's call. Lillian felt that precious time was often wasted that way. Besides, many people did not call a doctor when they did not have the money to pay. Mr. Schiff agreed with Lillian, and he arranged for doctors to make their services available through the United Hebrew Charities.

On her first day in the streets, Lillian noticed a little boy with red sore eyes, a symptom of a highly infectious eye disease. The boy disappeared into an old wooden tenement building, Number 7 Hester Street. Armed with a bottle of boric acid and clean cloths, Lillian went from one flat to another in search of the boy.

Number 7 Hester Street was a maze of tiny rooms. Open cans of garbage stood in the hallways. Lillian found a baby or a small child in need of special care in every flat. Every baby who lived in Number 7 Hester Street had a bath that day, and their mothers were given instructions on the importance of keeping their babies clean.

Lillian could almost taste the foul smell of the garbage that cluttered the narrow hallways. When she found a baby whose body was covered with rat bites, Lillian demanded that the janitor remove the garbage from the halls. Before Lillian left that house she found and treated the boy with the infected eyes, won the cooperation of the tenants, and frightened the janitor into a promise that the garbage would be taken out of the halls.

One night Lillian received a desperate call from the mother of a very sick child. The address was a tenement on Pearl Street. Pearl Street turned and twisted, making the address difficult to find. Dusk covered the city with darkening shadows. Lillian was walking down a deserted street near one of the extension arches of the Brooklyn Bridge. Three roughly dressed men were loitering under the arch. Lillian hesitated, and wondered if she should turn back and find a brighter street. But it was late already, and she did not know if she could find the way by herself.

"I am searching for this number on Pearl Street." Lillian spoke to one of the men and showed him the card with the address on it. "I don't know how to find it, I am a nurse and I have been called to care for a very sick child." Lillian fought back her fear of the men.

"Lady," said one of the men, "this ain't a very safe neighborhood for you and it's getting dark. We'll be glad to take you right to the address."

Two of the men walked with Lillian through the dark lonely streets, and one even held her case.

When they reached the address, Lillian thanked the men and went into the tenement. There was much to be done for the child, and Lillian stayed a long time. She came out into the dark moonless night to find that her escorts were still waiting. They did not leave her side until they came to the doorstep of the College Settlement.

The incident touched Lillian deeply, and she never forgot it. There was goodness in everyone; she would never doubt that.

Summer settled on the East Side in a great cloud of sweltering heat. Sleep in tiny bug-infested rooms was impossible. At all hours of the night, people could be

seen wearily dragging themselves toward the river,
where there was at least some hope of a breeze.

One night even Lillian, who usually fell quickly into a
deep, sound sleep, tossed and turned on her bed. Rubbing her aching arms, she gave up the struggle for sleep
that would not come, and sat by the window. Sleeping
children were everywhere, on the fire escapes, the hard
stone stoops, and even in the pushcarts that were left
standing on the streets.

As Lillian watched the sleepy stirrings of the children
on the street below, she thought of the summers she had
spent as a child. "These children do not even know there
is a seashore. They haven't ever seen a field of grass or
sat under a shady tree," she thought. "It's no wonder
that they grow up so fast. They are little old men and
ladies, exposed to the tragedies of life at an early age."

As a student nurse, Lillian had seen a precocious
awareness in even the youngest children. The memory of
two little girls crouched in a hospital corridor flashed
through her mind.

"Here come the Gerries," cried one. "Hide from them,
quick."

"Oh, they won't catch me," said the other. "I'm much
too fast."

The look of fright on the childrens' faces was much
too real for Lillian to guess that they were playing a
game.

"We didn't mean to give you a fright, Miss," said one
of the girls. "We were just playing a game."

"But who are the Gerries?" Lillian asked them.

"They are wicked people who come to take children

away from their fathers and mothers," the child explained.

"And they come when your mother is real sick and needs you," added the other.

Lillian found out later that the Gerries were the Society for the Prevention of Cruelty to Children.

"Ambulance" was another game that was played over and over again in the children's ward of the hospital. In this game, the ambulance usually came after there had been a fight on the street. Invariably, one of the players was "dying right on the street." Remembering the children's games, Lillian marveled at how accurately they often mirrored life on the East Side.

But what could you expect when children had no real fun, no sunny place to play for long and uninterrupted hours? Playgrounds on the East Side were the narrow alleys and heavily trafficked streets. Lillian was strongly tempted to join the College Settlement as a resident and work with Jane Robbins, Winifred Buck, and Jacob Riis. These people were deeply concerned with providing playgrounds for children, and a good fight had already begun. But Lillian was afraid to divert her energies. "First things first," she told herself. "There is a Nursing Service to be organized." Lillian felt that to be her first job.

Life at the College Settlement was exciting. It was the best way to be introduced to the neighborhood, and Lillian had no thought of losing her association with the dedicated social workers, who had become her friends. But to stay at the Settlement would inevitably mean to be part of its activities. Besides, the Settlement needed the space for the clubs and classes that were planned for the Fall. So Lillian and Mary decided to begin searching for a place of their own.

The nurses finally located a small apartment with an indoor bathroom on Jefferson Street. The apartment boasted a sitting room, a small dining room, and a kitchen. Up on the fifth floor, the windows were open to sunlight and an occasional breeze.

Lillian and Mary had a lot of fun decorating the apartment. They sewed white curtains, painted the floors, scrubbed down the walls, and accepted some good furniture from their parents' homes. The old Baltimore heater would serve them well in the cold winter months. Colorful pictures and favorite paintings added the final touch.

"Well now, this is just like home," said Lillian as she surveyed their handiwork.

"What do you mean, just like? It is home for us," laughed Mary.

"And it is to be a real home, too. A place where we live and a place where we work." Lillian was proud of the little flat.

Mary cooked the first meal. Lillian invited a little boy, who had watched them with fascination while they worked. The stew was rich with vegetables and gravy. But the little boy seemed gravely quiet all during the meal.

"He was so restless. He could hardly wait to leave," Lillian remarked when the little boy had gone.

"I wonder, didn't he like my cooking?" Mary asked.

"He must have. He ate every bit," said Lillian.

Soon there was a knock on the door. It was the little boy's mother, the janitress of the house, Mrs. McCrae.

"I just had to see for myself," she said smiling. "My lad came running downstairs, and he says to me, 'Them ladies live like the Queen of England. They eat off solid gold plates.' "

So, that's why he left so fast," said Mary, and invited Mrs. McCrae to come in and sit down.

4. Visiting Nurses

"*Who are those nurses?* Why are they snooping around?" people seemed to ask when they saw Lillian and Mary in their blue uniforms. The bright silver badge that read VISITING NURSES, UNDER THE AUSPICES OF THE BOARD OF HEALTH was scarcely understood.

"People treat us like strangers," said Lillian, wearily shrugging off her coat and tossing it onto the sofa.

"It's going to take a long time before people accept us. We'll just have to be patient." Mary had the endurance of a quiet faith to match the headstrong determination of her friend. Lillian had little patience for waiting.

"Even people who know us turn away when they see us on the street. They are afraid to greet us." Lillian was not as troubled by the fact that they had not yet had a single patient as she was by the apparent lack of explanation for this rejection.

"People have no reason to trust us, Lillian. We can't force them to call on us. Time will give us the chance to prove that we can help them," Mary said reassuringly.

"Of course, you're right. I'm not really surprised that people don't trust us. Everyone else seems to treat the immigrants so shabbily. What reason do they have to think we would treat them differently?" Lillian felt a new respect for her neighbors.

"My own impatience embarrasses me when I look at a newspaper. The foreign-born are being blamed for every crime that is taking place in the city. It's so unfair." Lillian held out the *New York World* to show Mary the screaming headline.

"Lillian, you always sound so dramatic," Mary gently chided her friend. "The newspaper isn't to blame for our difficulty. People are just afraid that we treat only charity patients. They have too much pride to admit that they need charity."

In her gentle way, Mary seemed to be able to go directly to the heart of the matter. With an understanding far beyond her years, Mary Brewster sensed how very much the newly arrived immigrants wanted to make a place for themselves in America. A very large number of the immigrants were Jews who had fled from persecution in Russia and Poland; almost all of them had fled from hunger and deprivation in the lands of their birth. They had come to America to make new lives for themselves, and to accept charity was to admit that they had failed.

"We are not giving them charity," said Lillian. From the very beginning Lillian and Mary had decided to charge a fee, however small. Sometimes they charged only ten cents, just so that people would feel free to call on them again and again. But most people did not know about the fee, and Lillian knew that she could not take money from those who had none to spare. No, it was going to take time to gain acceptance.

Thousands of immigrants were coming into the city, crowding the tenements, only to find that there was no work. Long lines of hungry people, men, women, and children, stood before the soup kitchens. And as disease often follows right behind hunger, an epidemic of typhoid fever struck the East Side with gale force. The fever swept over the neighborhood and struck victims in almost every home.

Lillian was in the hallway of a tenement when a man called to her. Through the open door, Lillian saw three children huddled in blankets on the floor. A woman was on her knees beside them, sobbing.

"Nurse, please help my children," the father pleaded.

"My babies are burning with fever, and the doctor hasn't come. We called him hours ago," the mother explained.

Lillian quickly removed the blankets and began to sponge the children with cold water. "This is to reduce the fever," she explained.

"Is that what I should have been doing? I could have killed by babies," the woman moaned. In that instant,

Lillian realized how important it was to explain to people how to care for their sick children.

"More lives could be saved if people knew what to do in an emergency," said Lillian. She and Mary made it a point to leave careful instructions with their patients.

Slowly, more and more people began to call upon the nurses. The VISITING NURSES, UNDER THE AUSPICES OF THE BOARD OF HEALTH had finally been accepted.

The nurses found people eager to learn how to care for the sick. "Treatment first, instruction second," Lillian and Mary agreed. But they encouraged their patients to feel free to call upon them.

It wasn't nearly so simple for Lillian to persuade her patients to go to the hospital. In their ignorance of such an institution, many people feared the hospital, convinced that it was a place where you went to die.

"If you go, you will protect your children, who must eat and sleep in the same room with you," Lillian explained over and over again. "You will receive care and medicines there that I do not have."

Fear was dispelled slowly. When the ambulance came, Lillian got on with her patients and held their hands. Slowly, her patients transferred their trust in Lillian to the hospital. They knew that the good nurse would not lie to them.

Lillian spent a lot of her time on the ambulance that winter, but her patients faced the hospital bravely—with new hope.

Over and over again, Lillian explained to her patients the danger of letting milk stand and thus spoil. Many of the immigrants had been peasants and farmers in the old country; they had lived on farms where there was little chance for fresh cows' milk to spoil.

"These women live in a city now. What they learned on a farm has little use here." Lillian began to demonstrate sterilization to the mothers of the East Side. She was able to get tickets for free ice, which she gave to her patients. The women learned to sterilize their babies' bottles and to keep the milk on ice. Their pale, sick babies began to grow strong . . . and their faith in the Visiting Nurses grew.

The job of nursing sick people in their homes taxed Lillian's ingenuity. She often marveled at what necessity forced her to invent. Clean clothes, rubber matting, and sterile sheets were scarce. The common ordinary newspaper, found in almost every home, became indispensable equipment. It was used under sheets to keep mattresses from staining; rolled up, it made an excellent wastebasket for soiled and contaminated cotton. Placed under sterile jars and bottles, the newspaper prevented contamination.

In the nurses' own apartment, chilly winter nights sent icy draughts of wind through the fifth floor flat; Lillian's fingers were almost too numb with cold to write. But she had promised to write reports to the President of the Board of Health. She wrapped a shawl around her shoulders and stuck her feet into the oven. With a pad of paper propped on her lap, Lillian wrote her report and a detailed account of her expenses for Jacob Schiff. It showed, penny by penny, where the money went: for eggs, milk, prescriptions, the rent by which some poor family was saved from eviction, or money to fix a pair of spectacles. And Lillian wrote of what she saw: "Enough sorrow, poverty and illness to fill a world with sadness."

Lillian tried to learn where jobs were available. And where there were none, she tried to persuade people to create them.

Lillian smiled at the official of the Health Department. "You ought to know how much better it is to restore a man's dignity than to give him charity," she said.

The official avoided looking into Lillian's eyes. "This nurse is a nuisance," he thought. Aloud, he said: "And what do you suggest, Miss Wald?"

"The streets are filthy. Why not hire people to sweep them," Lillian said calmly—she wasn't going to be brushed off.

"All right, Miss Wald, you have my permission to send people to my office. I'll see what I can do. But you do realize that we have a small budget. I can't make any promises." The official had a vision of his small office crowded with clamoring job seekers.

That very afternoon, Lillian gave one of her neighbors the address of the Board of Health. Although the neighbor was an extremely pious man, he was so desperate for work that he had shaved off his beard so that it might not hinder him from obtaining work. This was a very difficult thing for so religious a man to do. The next day, when Lillian passed him on the street, the man raised a smiling face in greeting and pointed proudly to his broom.

Frequently, Lillian found patients, sick with tubercu-

losis or smallpox, propped up in their beds sewing clothing. The next day those same garments were hanging in
a clothing store, ready to infect an unsuspecting pur-
chaser.

Lillian was shocked. "Those garments are a hazard to
the health of a whole city." Lillian had gone to her
friend, Jacob Riis, the courageous newspaperman who
had been crusading against the abuses of the home sweatshop.

But manufacturing could be done cheaply in the
home, and until the home sweatshop was outlawed, there
was very little that could be done in the way of preven-
tive action.

Sometimes as many as nine or ten people—men,
women, and children—worked in a tiny crowded apartment. The sweatshop bosses were immigrants themselves, men who had managed to buy a few sewing
machines.

"At least this way we do not starve," the people explained to Lillian. There was no other work. The sweatshop bosses often stood between the workers and actual
starvation.

Lillian was gradually made aware of the fact that
being a nurse was not enough. The health problems of
her neighbors were caused by the crowded living conditions, the dark, dank, hallways, the uncollected garbage.
Epidemics swept over the East Side after months of hunger and starvation, and the germs lingered. Lillian joined
the Social Reform Club with her old friends from the
College Settlement, "To sweep the city clean of corrup-

tion." Politics added a new dimension to Lillian's partic-
ipation in the life of her neighbors.

On New Year's Day, there was a knock on the door.

"We have come to celebrate with you, Miss Wald,"
said a chorus of voices. Lillian opened the door to her
smiling neighbors, who thrust their New Year's cards
into her hands. Lillian invited them all in for tea and
cake.

"I really feel like a neighbor now," Lillian said to
Mary when the company had gone. But as Lillian turned
toward her friend, she noticed for the first time how
really tired Mary looked.

"Mary, you're not looking well at all. Let me feel
your forehead. I bet you have a fever." Lillian was concerned. Mary always was slender, but now she appeared
too thin, and her small face was pinched.

"Oh, it's nothing," protested Mary, "probably the
effects of a winter cold."

"I've been noticing too. You are a lot thinner, Mary,"
said Mrs. McCrae. "You girls are so busy taking care of
everyone else that you just plain forget about your-
selves." The janitress had become very fond of the
nurses. More than anyone else, she knew the cost of the
nurses' work to themselves.

"I'm going to see to it that you girls get more rest and
eat your meals in peace and quiet. Somebody has got to
look after you, and that somebody is going to be me."
Mrs. McCrae nodded her head vigorously. She was true
to her word.

All visitors were kept away while the nurses were having their meals, and only the direst of emergencies could

interrupt their sleep. Mrs. McCrae moved upstairs where she could keep better watch over "her girls" and gave up the basement apartment, for which she did not have to pay rent.

Every Sunday, during that cold winter, Lillian and Mary took groups of children to the uptown parks. There were no parks or playgrounds on the lower East Side.

"I know where we can get a sled and find some wonderful snow-covered hills," Lillian told the children on their first trip uptown.

For the first time, Lillian and Mary opened the eyes of the East Side children to the beauty and magic of playing and sledding on the wide open snow-covered hills. Lillian became so enthusiastic about the Sunday excursions that she persuaded Jacob Schiff to provide more sleds. The excursions grew, and more and more children were invited to come along.

When the snow melted from the hills on Riverside Drive, the children were given balls and bats. But one bright Sunday afternoon, just after the boys had been divided into teams, a policeman came running. "What are you doing here?" he shouted. "Don't you know that ball playing is not allowed here?"

"There is just no place for these children to play," Lillian told Jacob Schiff sadly. On the whole lower East Side, there was only one place, and that was an old graveyard.

Thousands of new children were coming into the city. They were crowding into schools that had been built for much smaller populations. The schools were old, and much too small for all the children they had to accommodate. One school was so dark inside that the gas had to be kept burning on even the brightest days. And it was so cold that the children had to jump up and down to keep from shivering whenever the teacher opened a window to let in fresh air.

After meeting Jane Addams, and learning of the wonderful work of Hull House in Chicago, Lillian was inspired to plan a settlement house on the East Side.

"The first thing I'm going to have is a decent playground for the children," Lillian decided.

The nurses had outgrown the little flat on Jefferson Street, and the idea of a big house where they could have a real clinic seemed more and more desirable.

When Rosh Hashanah came, Lillian and Mary eagerly joined in the celebrations. Small gifts of fish and honey cake were brought to the nurses.

"Surely," Lillian thought, "the Jewish New Year should be a time of hope and a renewal of the spirit." Lillian watched as the lower East Side tried to take a vacation from its troubles.

Housewives scoured their tiny rooms, and prepared for the holidays as best they could. The older men in long black frock coats and little black caps spent the days in prayer in the little storefronts that served as their synagogues. The poverty and the suffering of Lillian's neighbors was temporarily overshadowed by the glory and dignity of the holiday.

Lillian could not help but notice how wide the gap was becoming between the foreign born and their children. "The ways of the fathers must seem very out of place to the young." Lillian had often wondered what would happen to the heritage of the Jewish immigrant, who knew the ancient wisdom of the Torah by heart, but whose son all too often knew only the wisdom of the street. Eager to shed their foreign ways, the younger generation sometimes went too far, mocking their elders, who held steadfast to their old customs and observances.

Meanwhile, Mary began to cough more. Her blonde curls seemed to make too large a frame for her face, which had the fragile china look that tuberculosis often gave its victims.

"You have got to rest more, Mary. You're working much too hard." Lillian was really worried, and she wrote a long letter to Mr. Brewster, Mary's father, asking him to come and take Mary home, where she could get the rest she so desperately needed.

"In a few months you'll be back. Just wait and see," Lillian called to Mary, waving till the carriage that was taking Mary Brewster home was out of sight.

Mary had tuberculosis, as Lillian had feared, and she never regained her strength. She was never to know the fruits her pioneer efforts were to bear.

When Mr. Brewster wrote to tell Lillian of Mary's death, Lillian was deeply shaken. "The very least I can do is go on with the work we both began." Lillian made a silent promise that Mary's work would be remembered, and she worked harder than ever.

Lillian was always able to draw comfort from her work. The time had come, she decided, for VISITING NURSES, UNDER THE AUSPICES OF THE BOARD OF HEALTH to grow.

Lillian wrote to Annie Goodrich, a young nurse who

had worked with her at the New York Hospital, asking her to come and join the service. Lillian had confidence in the bright, friendly girl.

Soon after Annie Goodrich joined Lillian, Lavinia Dock and Lina Rogers also became Visiting Nurses. The three young nurses were quick to recognize the challenge that Lillian had named "Public Health Nursing."

Public Health Nursing was proving its value on the lower East Side, but doctors and nurses, trained for work in the hospital, had still to be persuaded that many illnesses could be properly cared for in the home.

Lillian's work had taken her deep into the life of the lower East Side, and Mr. Schiff quietly searched for a large house where her dream of clinic, settlement house, and playground could come true.

5. School Nurse

Lillian loved the old mansion on Henry Street the very minute she set eyes on its lovely stone front. Rich brown wood panelling covered the walls and gave elegance to the house.

"It reminds me of my old home in Rochester," Lillian told Jacob Schiff as he led her through the rooms. Mr. Schiff breathed a sigh of relief; Lillian was pleased. It had taken him a long time to find a house on the lower East Side that would be suitable for the Nurses' Settlement.

Lillian began to plan each room as she walked through the old house, and Jacob Schiff agreed to make the alterations she suggested.

Lillian bought comfortable chairs and sofas, and long,

colorful drapes for the windows. On the first floor were the clinic and the office of the Visiting Nurses Association.

"It is really a bit of glory on the lower East Side, a place for neighbors to visit with one another in comfort." Lillian described the house in a letter to her mother.

"Best of all," she wrote, "is the playground."

Purple, red, and yellow flowers made a gay border around the playground. Shiny new benches were put under the shade of the ailanthus tree, near the swings, the parallel bars, and an overhead ladder. A brightly colored awning shaded the sandpile. And when Lillian saw an old-fashioned hurdy gurdy in a store window, she could not resist buying it for the play area.

From the very first day, the playground was open to the children of the neighborhood. It was never empty. At all times of the day, it was filled with laughing, playing children.

"It was an inspiration to put the hurdy gurdy out there." Lillian laughed, as she watched Lavinia pass through the play yard and go out of her way to give the hand organ an extra turn.

The brightness of the play yard was like an oasis of sunlight in the midst of the grimy, broken houses that cluttered the streets and alleys of the East Side.

There were a million and a half people in New York City in 1890, and more than a quarter of a million were crowded into the lower East Side of Manhattan.

Visiting Nurses had grown to five nurses, and they

often felt helpless against wave after wave of smallpox, typhoid fever and tuberculosis which infected the neighborhood.

One evening, Annie Goodrich, who usually entertained the dinner table with her bright chatter, was strangely silent. Suddenly she tossed her napkin aside, nearly overturning a glass of water, and began shouting angrily.

"Lillian, I think we are wasting our time. We nurses are simply no match for the filth and garbage that fills the hallways of every tenement around here." Annie's voice was strained with tension.

"It's hopeless, just hopeless. The bottle of disinfectant that you insist we leave in every home does about as much good as pouring a glass of water on a raging fire," Annie shouted at Lillian.

"I don't see why these people want to come here. Yet hundreds of immigrants come every day, with their golden dreams and ragged clothes, to live in more cramped and suffocating conditions than herrings packed in a barrel." Annie spoke more quietly now; her anger was spent.

"It's a wonder that anybody at all escapes sickness, living in these conditions," Lillian said softly. "But let's remember that we are nurses. Our job is to do as much as we can. We are not here to judge these people; we're here to help them." Lillian had learned Miss Sutliffe's lessons on discipline well. Good discipline among the nurses was part of good morale. And a good morale was a sure sign that the nurses were doing their work well.

"We have to try anything and everything, no matter

how much time it takes." Lillian spoke firmly. "It isn't a losing battle. Why don't you look at what we have accomplished, instead of what we haven't? Lillian reminded the nurses of how they had managed to convince a group of mothers to try cooking inexpensive but nutritious green vegetables for their families.

Lillian had invited a few of the women to come to a meeting at the Settlement House.

At first the women had been ill-at-ease and suspicious. Somehow, Lillian had realized, she would have to take their minds off their awkwardness, so that they could relax and begin to speak freely with one another. A sudden inspiration told her to tell them about the fire that had taken place the day before, and how one of the nurses had narrowly escaped from the burning building.

Chins dropped and eyes brightened. The room was deathly quiet when Lillian finished speaking. And then all of a sudden, everyone began to speak at once. One of the women told of a narrow escape she herself had made.

"So many terrible things," said one of the women, shaking her head from side to side. "You never know what is going to happen next." As the women talked together they relaxed, and no longer felt so uncomfortable and ill-at-ease.

Lillian invited them to come into the kitchen to watch a vegetable dish being prepared. Every one was served a portion. When the dish had been eaten and enjoyed, the women expressed their desire to take the recipe home.

"Sometime you'll let me make my favorite recipe," one of the women told Lillian.

"Everyone will have a turn. We'll be a real club and learn more about cooking and sewing," suggested another.

Lillian smiled. These women were so eager to learn, and they had so much to teach.

The members of the Mothers' Club, as they decided to call themselves, left the Settlement House filled with the good time they had had. Those funny greens had a good taste after all.

The women learned to take a new pride and interest in their cooking, and they tried the new foods that cost so little, and yet had so much nutrition.

The Mothers' Club met every week now. Step by step, these women were learning to make their lives better.

Annie had to admit that Lillian was right, but she couldn't help chiding the chief nurse: "It's good to be able to let off steam, too, even if it does provoke a lecture from you, Lillian."

Lillian laughed, "Right you are, and don't I sizzle like a hot iron whenever I have anything to do with the President of the Board of Health."

Ever since Lillian had known twelve-year-old Louis, she had been pleading with the Board of Health to put doctors into the schools.

Louis was a sad-eyed boy who wanted more than anything else to go to school.

"They won't let me into the schoolroom, Miss Wald,"

Louis explained to Lillian. "It's this rash on my head. Whenever a teacher sees it, she sends me right home."

The rash on Louis' head turned out to be a simple eczema. Lillian gave Louis an ointment and showed him how to rub it into his scalp. The rash soon cleared.

Lillian never forgot the radiant smile on Louis' face the first day he went back to school and wasn't sent home again. "It's all on account of you, Miss Wald," Louis had said, beaming at the nurse.

From then on Lillian wrote down the names of all children who were kept out of school for medical reasons. The list grew rapidly, and it included the names of both sick and handicapped children. Most of the children had only simple skin disorders. But Lillian felt that they all had the right to some kind of schooling.

"Do you know the heartbreak it is to some of these families when their children are not allowed to go to school?" Lillian had asked the President of the Board of Health.

"There is nothing I can do about it. I have enough work to do without worrying about the schools. Go and bother the Board of Education, Miss Wald." The offical of the Board of Health had turned away from Lillian, pretending to be very busy.

"It is your job," Lillian had insisted. "What's to be done about the children who would be in school, if only they had the necessary treatment? Besides, even if you don't think the schooling of children is your concern, surely you must want to prevent further contagion. What about the children in school with tuberculosis or small-pox, who don't know they are infecting others? They don't even know that they are sick. No one seems to even care," Lillian commented impatiently.

"Look, Miss Wald. There are simply no funds for the kind of medical service you propose, and I certainly am not here to hold the hand of every immigrant whose child happens to get sick. Good day, Miss Wald," the President said crisply, waving his arm as if to shoo Lillian away.

The City Administration was indifferent to the sufferings of the lower East Side. The Board of Health was doing practically nothing to control the spread of disease, but Lillian was determined not to give up.

"I'll be here again," she said calmly. "Your bad manners will not keep me from making my reports or letting you know what great work could be done."

Lillian knew it would take something drastic to convince the President of the Board of Health. He was a physician himself, but so backward and narrow-minded that he knew and cared little about public health. He had once been heard to ask, "Koch, who is this man Koch?" He was ignorant even of the great scientist who had identified the bacillus that causes tuberculosis.

One afternoon, Lillian was passing by the schoolyard, when she heard the excited screams of a crowd of children. As she came closer, she saw that the children were huddled in a close circle around a little boy, who was showing them how he could peel the skin from his arms.

"That boy has smallpox," Lillian gasped, and dashed into the schoolyard to pull the boy away from his friends.

Lillian took little Joey firmly by the arm and marched him straight to the office of the Board of Health. Lillian wasted no time. She did not even knock on the door of the President's office.

The President looked up from his desk. "Yes, Miss Wald, what is it today?" he asked, making no effort to conceal the annoyance in his voice.

"Sir, I have something that I'm sure you will be interested in seeing," said Lillian, struggling to keep her own voice calm.

"Joey, please show this man what you were showing the children in the schoolyard," said Lillian, turning to the scared little boy standing beside her.

Joey held out his arm and began to peel the skin. The President's eyes bulged when he saw what Joey was doing. He jumped up from his desk and shouted, "Get that boy out of my office. He has smallpox. What exactly are you doing, Miss Wald?" he asked angrily.

Lillian bit her lip; she refused to be intimidated by the shouting of an angry man. "If there had been medical supervision in the schools, Joey's smallpox would have been spotted before he had a chance to infect other children. He would not have been attending school every day."

The President fidgeted; he could hardly wait until Joey was out of his office.

"You have convinced me," he said, lowering his voice. "But now, please, get that boy out of my office."

As Lillian walked Joey home, she told him, "You are a real hero, Joey. You helped me win a big battle with the Board of Health."

If Joey had felt like a hero when he was showing off to his friends, he felt like a real grown-up hero now. Hadn't the nurse told him so? And Joey agreed to stay home from school until his skin stopped peeling.

"That man," protested Lillian, referring to the President of the Board of Health. "He can make the best plan practically useless."

One hundred and fifty doctors had been hired to examine the children in school, but they only had to be in the schools one hour each day. "What can they do in an hour?" Lillian was very disappointed with the new medical inspection plan.

"It does have one advantage," Lavinia was grinning. One hundred and fifty doctors can now make thirty dollars more a month than they could without the new inspection plan."

Lavinia's humor was lost on Lillian. "Oh Docky," Lillian shook her head in dismay. "How can a doctor even get interested in the school children? He no sooner takes off his hat than the hour is up. And besides, how can a person care about a job that expects so little?"

An effective plan of medical inspection in the schools had to wait until a new city administration was elected.

The city was waking up to the corruption at City Hall. New political clubs were forming in every neighborhood and the voters were aroused. In 1902, a new reform administration was voted into office. Seth Low was elected the city's new Mayor; Theodore Roosevelt was appointed the new Police Commissioner; and Dr. Lederle, a physician, was the new Commissioner of Health.

When Dr. Lederle took office, the first thing he did was to reform the medical inspection in the schools. The school doctors began to work three hours a day in the schools instead of only one.

Every child attending school was given a complete medical examination, and a medical record was kept for each child. Statistics began to be compiled and the city took a look at its own health.

Trachoma, a serious eye disease, was found to be very common among school children of the lower East Side. Thousands of children were sent home. Where the medical inspection was the most thorough, the schools were almost empty.

"Your doctors are doing too good a job," Lillian told Dr. Lederle. "But what good is sending children out of the classrooms, if they meet their classmates on the street and infect them there?" she asked.

The Commissioner agreed with Lillian, "When we began our examinations, we had no idea that we would see this much illnesss. But what can we do? Our job is to keep infection from spreading inside the schools. There is not much we can do when the children are outside."

"If there were nurses on your staff, follow-up treatment could be given. That way we would be sure that the infections are being treated," Lillian suggested.

Dr. Lederle hesitated. "I'm not sure that would be a good idea. Classes might be disturbed, and besides, don't you think people would rather bring their children to their own private physicians?"

"Not many people around here have their own private physicians," Lillian quickly replied. "Most of these children will go without any treatment at all, unless the Department of Health will provide it," she explained, surprised that Dr. Lederle knew so little about the people of the lower East Side.

"School nurses would be invaluable. They could keep epidemics from becoming so widespread." Lillian added, "Oh, Dr. Lederle, these children have a right to good health."

Lillian began to talk more quickly as an idea took shape in her mind. She was sure that the Commissioner would not refuse her request when he heard her entire plan.

"Our Henry Street nurses will pay the salary of a nurse, who will work under your direction, in the schools that you designate. Once you see what she can accomplish, I'm sure you will be convinced of the advantages of having nurses in all the schools." Lillian stopped and waited tensely for the Commissioner to reply.

Dr. Lederle smiled at Lillian, "Well, it certainly won't hurt to try. You select the nurse, and tell her to come to my office."

Dr. Lederle was willing to give the nurses a chance. He was an honest man with an open mind, and Lillian felt very grateful.

"Good luck," the Commissioner called as Lillian left his office.

"Who is going to be the first school nurse?" Lillian wondered, as she walked quickly back to Henry Street. Every one of the Henry Street nurses was enthusiastic about the plan. They all wanted to be the first School Nurse.

"I guess the only fair way is to draw straws," Lillian said, laughing, as she went to get the straws.

Lina Rogers was the lucky nurse. She had picked the straw that was to make her the first nurse to work in the New York City public schools.

Every day, Lina made the rounds of four schools on the lower East Side treating minor infections and bruises. Often the only space made available to her was in hallways or small, out-of-the-way rooms. Lina never complained about the inadequacy of a treating room, but went about her work quietly and unobtrusively.

Lina got the names of the children who had been sent home from the school doctors. Within one month, she had given 893 treatments and visited 137 homes.

Dr. Lederle stood in the office of the Henry Street Settlement, holding his hat in his hand. Lillian was surprised to see the Commissioner at Henry Street.

"I hope nothing has gone wrong," she said.

"Wrong, Miss Wald! It couldn't be more right. I came here to tell you the news myself." Dr. Lederle smiled broadly.

"The Board of Estimate has voted thirty thousand dollars to be used to pay the salaries of twelve school nurses. They will be the first nurses in the city to be on the payroll outside of the hospital wards." Dr. Lederle laughed. "It seems that you have not only convinced me, Miss Wald, but the Board of Estimate as well. Your nurse, Miss Rogers, has proven that nurses do indeed have a place in our schools. Personally, I think Miss Rogers has done a magnificent job."

"I'm not surprised that we have proven our point. But

I couldn't be more delighted that the Board of Estimate has acted so quickly." Lillian shook Dr. Lederle's proffered hand. "I think we have you to thank for that."

But there were other children, too, who were kept out of the classrooms. These were the slow learners, the mentally retarded. Elizabeth Farrell, a teacher who lived at Henry Street and taught at one of the neighborhood schools, was sure these children could learn, too. Lillian helped Elizabeth Farrell to convince the Board of Education to give her the chance to teach these children in a special class. The class was a success.

"There's a remedy for most of the ills of this world, if someone will only take the trouble to find it," Lillian noted in her diary.

"Spring is coming. I can feel it in the air," Lillian said gaily. "It must be glorious in the country. Why can't we take the children on a picnic to Sunset Hill?" Lillian impetuously planned a picnic for that very afternoon near the country house that had been given to the nurses as a convalescent home for patients.

Jacob Schiff brought his buggy to the Settlement House and the children piled in. When they reached the country house, the little hill was bathed in an orange light. The children watched the play of orange light against the sky with hungry expressions on their faces. It was as if they were drinking in the beauty of the sunset with their eyes.

"People can be starved for beauty as for food," Lillian said quietly to Jacob Schiff.

"Wouldn't it be wonderful if these children were able

to spend summers in the country?" Lillian asked, breathing in the cool air, free of the grime of the city.

Jacob Schiff sighed. Lillian had another plan, and he wondered just how long it would take her to see this one through.

The following summer, the Settlement House boasted two summer camps, one for girls and one for boys.

6. "Eat 'Em Alive," Grand Annual Ball

Lillian felt a curious mixture of exhilaration and melancholy as she walked down the tree-lined street in Rochester, where she had spent her childhood.

This was Lillian's first visit to Rochester since the Nurses' Settlement had been opened. At first she had been much too busy to take time off for a visit with her family. And then she kept putting it off. Lillian's sister Julia and her husband had expressed disapproval of Lillian's plans, and Lillian had tried to avoid the inevitable arguments.

Lillian stopped in front of the old famliy home. The gracious mansion no longer belonged to the Wald family. It had been sold soon after Max Wald's death, when Minnie had decided to move into Julia's house.

It was strange, Lillian thought, not to think of the lovely old house as home. It was just as beautiful as she remembered, and it was home for so many wonderful memories.

"Well, it isn't home any more," Lillian said half aloud as she walked on to Julia's. "The house on Henry Street is just as dear to me now as that old house used to be."

But when Julia opened the door and Lillian stepped inside, she did feel that she had come home.

"It's just like old times," Lillian said, looking at the smiling faces hovering over her. There was her mother, Julia and Charles, and her younger brother Gus, who had become a successful young businessman.

After dinner, the entire family sat around Julia's luxurious parlor and listened to Lillian tell about life on New York's lower East Side.

"Come and visit," Lillian encouraged, "I promise you an exciting time."

"From your descriptions of life on Henry Street, I hardly doubt that," put in Charles Barry.

"But what about you, Lillian? Don't you have any personal life at all?" asked Julia.

There were so many challenges, so many things waiting to be done, that Lillian had no time or even thought of a life apart from the nurses and the Settlement.

"Aren't you even thinking of marriage?" Julia was relentless. Marriage had filled her life, and she could not understand how any woman could be happy unless she was married and had a family. It simply did not seem right to Julia for her pretty, spirited sister to be living a spinster's life.

Lillian shook her head. "My life is hardly empty, you know. I certainly don't think of myself as a spinster," Lillian laughed, reading Julia's thoughts. "But now that I think of it, the word does fit."

"You used to have so many male admirers," Julia persisted. But Lillian was having trouble keeping a straight face.

"Here I am feeling sorry for you, and you just sit there laughing," said Julia helplessly.

"I'm sorry Julia. But don't be too harsh with me. I agree that marriage is a wonderful thing. It simply hasn't happened. But, please, don't feel sorry for me. I'm a very happy woman and more than content with my life," Lillian said, noting the look of embarrassed confusion on Julia's face.

"Really Julia, I'm not against men or matrimony. I'm just an upside down sort of person. I find my life fun and filled with surprises. My friends are my family," Lillian said seriously.

"I still don't understand you," said Julia. "And I probably never will. But I only spoke for your own good. I'm still your older sister." And then Julia smiled. "As long as you're happy, I won't bring up the subject again."

"Still the same Julia, my big bossy sister." Lillian got up from her chair to give Julia a hug.

"Lillian, it's really good to have you home," Julia said softly. "Things get a little depressing sometimes. Mother gets very blue and sort of at odd ends."

"I wonder if she'd like the change of a visit to Henry Street. It would be nice to have her," Lillian suggested.

Minnie Wald had led a busy and active life, and Lillian was sure she would like the Settlement House.

At first Minnie was reluctant. She loved the serenity of Julia's spacious home, and she was used to a quiet neighborhood. But Lillian finally persuaded her to come and give the Settlement House a try.

It did not take Minnie Wald very long to feel at home in the Nurses' Settlement. Sitting on the little veranda that jutted from Lillian's window, Minnie remarked how very much the house on Henry Street reminded her of the old family home in Rochester.

"It's warm and friendly, but it's elegant, too," Minnie Wald said, leaning back in her chair. She was thoroughly enjoying becoming a part of the Henry Street family. Her lively nature wakened in the bustle of people coming and going, which was as much a part of the Settlement House as the downstairs clinic.

Minnie Wald basked in Lillian's popularity and quietly admired her daughter's way of persuading people to do her bidding without making demands or overwhelming them.

Charles Evans Hughes, who was soon to become Governor of New York State, Josephine Shaw Lowell, Jane Addams, Jacob Schiff, poets, writers, artists, doctors, famous people from all walks of life, were frequent guests at the dinner table. The conversation was sparkling as the food was good. In the dining room of the Nurses' Settlement, Minnie Wald felt as if she had a window looking out on the whole world.

Since she loved every minute of her visit at the Settlement, Minnie told Lillian that she wanted to make the Settlement House her home. Lillian was overjoyed. Her mother was much too vivacious a woman to stay in retirement. Lillian was not one bit surprised to learn that Minnie was determined to take an active part in Settlement House life.

Lillian would never have noticed the yellow paper that lay on the steps of the Settlement House, if the wind had not whirled it around and dropped it right in front of her. The large black letters caught her eye. She picked up the paper and read the handbill:

> "EAT 'EM ALIVE," Grand Annual Ball
> Saturday night
> sponsored by the American Heroes of the
> Henry Street Settlement

Lillian was surprised. "The boys never mentioned that they were holding a dance. I wonder why?" She mused. "They probably thought I wouldn't approve."

But she was wrong. The American Heroes was the name of the Boys' Club of the Henry Street Settlement. Lillian had organized the club and the boys wanted to show her their appreciation. Someone had told them that Lillian needed a writing desk, and they wanted to surprise her with a new one. If it weren't for Miss Wald, they felt, the American Heroes would never have become a real club, with a place to meet at the Settlement.

Lillian herself never forgot the eventful night that the Boys' Club was founded.

One night, at dinner, the most awful sounds were

heard through the open window. Wolf howls, the hard clang of garbage cans being turned over, and raucous laughter filled the room.

"That's the last straw," Lillian had said, getting up from the table.

In the dim light of the lamppost, Lillian saw the rubbish piled on the steps of the Settlement House. Down the street were the figures of running boys.

"Harry," Lillian called, knowing that where there was mischief, Harry was sure to be a part of it.

Harry emerged from out of the shadows.

"Harry," said Lillian, "Call back your friends and clean up this awful mess. And when you're finished, come inside. I want to talk to all of you."

"Yes ma'am," the boy whispered almost inaudibly. There was something about Miss Wald that made him take the broom she held out to him. It wasn't that she was scolding. No, her voice wasn't loud. It was the unaccustomed firmness that caught Harry off guard.

Lillian went back inside, but not before she heard Harry calling to his friends.

"Those boys are a nuisance, simply because they have nothing else to do," Lillian said to the people at the dinner table.

"It's time we got the boys together into a club. If only there were someone to supervise them." Lillian looked hopefully at Herbert Lehman, a young university student who had just come to live at the Settlement House in order to study the economic conditions of the lower East Side.

"I'd be glad to help. I could teach the boys baseball

and boxing," offered Herbert, who was to become both Governor and Senator of the State of New York.

"That's wonderful," Lillian said happily. "We already have a Girls' Club, and now we'll have a Boys' Club too." She could hardly wait to tell the boys, who were busy cleaning the steps.

Before long eight unkempt boys, with arms hanging out of too-short shirt sleeves, eyes lowered, and faces blank of expression, filed into the Settlement House. They were ready for the long lecture they were sure was to come. No one dared look up. If they had, they would have relaxed, because they would have seen the wide smile on Lillian's face.

"How would you boys like to be the first Henry Street Boys' Club?" Lillian asked, and introduced Herbert Lehman to the boys.

"Mr. Lehman will teach you boxing and baseball, and you can have a room in the Settlement House for your meetings."

One of the boys whistled. "Gee, Miss Wald, that would be great. Some of the other fellows in the neighborhood would want to come too," he said enthusiastically.

The boys called the new club the American Heroes.

"It's a good name," Lillian agreed when the boys told her. They needed an important sounding name, because they felt so unimportant.

"Everyone needs to feel like a somebody, especially a lonely boy, who feels like a nobody," Lillian thought, hoping that the club would help the boys to feel that people really did care.

The American Heroes was an immediate success. New members joined every day.

But now Lillian frowned as she read the announcement. The dance would surely become a brawl if it was held in a dance hall on the Bowery.

The Bowery, with its red and green blinking neon lights, was a magnet which drew young people looking for excitement. One tavern was right next to the other, and from each doorway dance music blared, mingling with the sound of drunken laughter.

Unfortunately, these halls were too easy to rent for a dance or any other affair. The rent was cheap, because the managers knew they could make money from the sale of cheap liquor.

"Eat 'Em Alive" Annual Ball was to be held in a tavern that was known as Suicide Hall, because a murder had been committed there.

"Perhaps the bartender will agree to keep the bar closed that night," Lillian thought. Wrapping her coat tightly around her to protect her from the cold wind, Lillian headed for the Bowery and Suicide Hall.

"Lady," said the sleepy bartender, "if I closed down my bar, I'd lose all my regular customers, and then I'd be out of a job."

Lillian nodded her head. "Of course," she said sadly. It had been silly to even ask, but she had had to try.

The "Eat 'Em Alive" Grand Annual Ball took place the next night. Suicide Hall was packed with young people. Inside, the smoke was so thick that Lillian could barely make out their faces. A strong whiskey smell filled the air with an acrid aroma. Lillian almost choked

on the sour odor. She could neither move further in nor out again. Someone pressed a heel into her toe and Lillian winced at the pain. The crowd surged forward, carrying the nurse in with them.

Lillian finally managed to push her way out, back into fresh air. "Whew," she sighed in relief, and breathed the air hungrily.

"That's the last time the Henry Street Boys' Club is going to hold a dance in a beer hall," Lillian told Jacob Schiff the very next night.

"My dear young lady," said Mr. Schiff, "you've convinced me. But you must admit that you are a most expensive dinner guest." Mr. Schiff laughed and signed the check for a down payment on a social hall.

The generous financier was quick to see that a social hall would be a good investment, and he was sure that other businessmen would want to have a share in it. "You have had many good plans, Lillian, but this is the first one that shows your skill in business," Jacob Schiff said admiringly.

Clinton Hall, as the new social hall was named, was designed for the people on the lower East Side. It was a place where dances and celebrations could be held in dignity and in wholesome surroundings.

The Hall had rooms suitable for weddings, bar mitzvahs and dances. There was an auditorium, a ballroom, recreation rooms, dining halls, and kitchens that were specially equipped for the preparation of kosher meals. There was also a roof garden with a real stage for dramatic performances. Clinton Hall was the first building of its kind on the East Side.

Lillian's schedule was hectic. Up at six every morning, she hardly ever got to bed before midnight. There was always so much to do.

Between the Visiting Nurses Service and the Settlement House, Lillian could never get away for more than a week at a time. And when she did, she rushed back to Henry Street at the earliest opportunity. She hated to be away.

The Mothers' Club, the Boys' Club and the Girls' Social Club met regularly. One by one, new classes were started in Art, Music and Dance. New horizons were opened to hundreds of East Side children; there was a country house, and a summer camp. At the Settlement a boy or girl could learn a musical instrument, or learn to draw and paint, or act on the stage. And what was the most heartening to Lillian was that here the spirit had a chance to breathe and grow.

Lillian always chose her nurses and teachers carefully. Those who were interested only in themselves or felt superior to other people were not welcome to work at the Settlement. Lillian wanted people who really cared about other people.

One afternoon, a young social worker came to the Settlement House on assignment from her class at College.

Lillian asked the girl to look in on an unmarried mother who lived next door to the Settlement to see how she was feeling.

"Is she an interesting case?" the young social worker asked, hoping to learn something more about the girl.

"What do you mean, case?" Lillian became impatient. "People are not cases. I asked you to see how a poor lonely girl is feeling, and you talk about an interesting case. We deal with people here, not psychology lessons," Lillian told the embarrassed young student.

7. Children at Work

The call came early in the afternoon, and Lillian rushed to the laundry on Ludlow Street. A boy lay unconscious on the grimy floor of the large commercial laundry. Lillian took one look at his crushed arm, and gasped, "What happened, how could he have mangled his arm like that?"

"It was the press, Miss, see." The man pointed to a large metal machine. "I guess it was too heavy for a skinny kid to handle," he explained.

Lillian barely heard the man; she was too busy working on the prone figure of the boy. "He's going to lose his arm, there's no way to save it. And if we're going to save him, we must get him to the hospital at once." Lillian did what she could for the boy until the ambulance arrived.

When the boy was safely in the ambulance, Lillian turned back into the laundry. She was not going to leave until she found out from the boss why so young a boy was working the dangerous machine.

"It was his job," said the boss. "He should have been more careful."

But why do you hire young children to work the heavy machines?" Lillian scrutinized the short stout man, who began to fidget under her steady gaze.

"The boy's father is dead. I was doing the family a favor by giving him a job."

"I hardly think the boy's mother is going to think you were helping her when she finds out what happened to her son. That boy will be crippled for the rest of his life." Lillian spoke accusingly.

Lillian left the laundry with a heavy heart. Her steps were slow as she walked back to Henry Street. She passed the schoolhouse just as the children were being dismissed for the day.

Hundreds of children poured out of the doors. The children came running—jumping, pushing and laughing. Little faces, pale and thin, rosy and chubby, smiling, serious, dark, fair, blonde, brunette, jostled past Lillian.

"They are a whole world in miniature. And where else but on the East Side can such lively crowds be found?" Lillian thought wonderingly.

"Children have a right to be protected." Lillian reminded herself of the boy at the laundry.

Children of all ages could be found in the laundries, the bakeries, groceries, and factories of the lower East Side, as well as in the home sweatshops.

Where was it to end? How was this cruelty to be stopped? What kind of a future awaited children who were kept from going to school?

The streets were full of home sweatshops. Lillian knew too well how hopeless it was to convince hungry people that they were cruelly exploiting their children.

"We can barely keep ourselves from starving as it is," one of Lillian's patients had explained. With the children working, the man was able to pay his rent.

When Lillian had lived on Jefferson Street, she had only to look out of the window of her flat to be reminded of the sweatshop. In almost every window across the way, she could see people bent over their machines. There was one family in particular that seemed to work around the clock; no matter how early Lillian got up or how late she went to bed, this family could be seen seated at their machines.

"It is impossible to regulate the sweatshops," an inspector had once complained to Lillian. "People have become so secretive, that when I come to check on their licenses I feel as if I'm taking the bread right out of their mouths."

Lillian nodded her head, thinking of the many times work had been hidden under beds and tables when a nurse was expected. More than once, Lillian had seen one of her child patients hastily stuffing a half-finished pair of trousers or a blouse under the pillow or the bed.

But Lillian had also seen the shame in the eyes of the mothers and fathers.

"Is it a sin to work?" they seemed to ask. "We have to

live. We don't want our children taken away from us and put into orphan homes because we can't make enough money to keep our families together."

Lillian had tried to be sympathetic. Poverty placed terrible burdens upon these people. It was futile to blame the parents.

When Florence Kelley came to live at the Henry Street Settlement, Lillian's first serious efforts against Child Labor began.

Florence Kelley came to New York from Hull House in Chicago. Her job as factory inspector in the state of Illinois had given her first-hand knowledge of factories and sweatshops. The abolition of child labor had become the driving force in Florence's life when her father, a Congressman from Pennsylvania, had taken her on an inspection of a steel factory.

The sight of bare-backed children working with acids that blistered and scarred their hands was etched deeply in the memory of young Florence, whose interest in social work had begun at that very moment.

"It would be a whole lot easier for men to find jobs if it were not so cheap to hire women and children. Children are very cheap labor." Florence Kelley spoke in a crisp direct way, her face animated by a quick smile. But when she was angry, her eyes seemed to flash sparks of green fire. The slim, red-headed woman had become a champion of exploited children. Her anger and determination were tempered by a real knowledge of the economics of factory production. Florence Kelley had become an expert on the plight of children in the trades.

Florence Kelley and Lillian Wald established the Child

Labor Committee. The work of the new committee took Lillian away from the Settlement House more and more, until she found it impossible to give the necessary time to the supervising of the Visiting Nurses Service.

"I think it is time for me to step down as head nurse and give Annie Goodrich the job," Lillian announced one evening.

The decision was a sound one, and Annie accepted the job. Lillian was now free to travel around the country with Florence Kelley.

"Before we can fight, we need the facts in black and white," Florence said at the first meeting of the Committee on Child Labor. Facts and figures always impress the lawmakers."

Florence and Lillian traveled from state to state and city to city. They visited factories, reform schools, orphanage asylums, and they spoke to teachers, doctors, and judges. And what they learned made their hair stand on end.

To their horror they discovered thousands of children in the textile factories of the South and New England, and in the silk mills of Pennsylvania.

"At least a quarter of those children are under the age of sixteen," Lillian said, horrified.

There were children in the coal mines, the steel mills, and in the railroad yards. They worked on cotton plantations and in the orchards. And very often they worked from dawn to dusk.

"The more states we visit, the uglier the facts become," Lillian remarked to Florence when they were leaving a glass factory that was fenced in with barbed wire to keep the little boy workers from escaping at night.

"We have even seen children chained to machines to keep them working. Where do these children come from? Surely children who have families would not be treated this way!" Lillian discovered that these children were taken out of orphan homes and reform schools.

"Their only guardian is the state . . . and too often, the state isn't even aware of their existence," Lillian learned.

"Some of these states don't even keep records of birth. It's impossible to get population statistics from them." Florence threw up her hands in anger. "It seems we'll have to pull some of these states up out of the Middle Ages—where they have been for the last hundred years."

Back home in the tiny cubicle that served as the office of the Child Labor Committee, Florence and Lillian went over the figures carefully and painstakingly.

"Have you noticed how many boys who used to sell newspapers are now serving jail sentences?" Florence wrinkled her nose in that funny way she had when she was busy thinking about something.

It seemed to be an amazing coincidence. Florence Kelley had her suspicions, but before they reached any conclusions, Florence and Lillian wanted to hear the boys tell their own stories.

That very afternoon, the two women visited the New York Juvenile Asylum, where Florence's suspicions were quickly confirmed. Boy after boy told the same story of an offer of easy money, and the threat of harm if they did not do as they were told.

The underworld had claimed its victims, the unwary newsboys, on the dark streets. These boys sold their papers in front of the saloons, the pool halls, and cheap hotels. Promised a big reward and threatened with the alternative of a beating, boys as young as seven and eight rushed to carry out the wicked errand that sooner or later sent them to the New York Juvenile Asylum.

"It's no wonder," Lillian told the Committee. "Look at the hours those boys kept and the places where they worked. They probably earned more on one errand than in a whole year of selling newspapers."

The facts came together one by one, unfolding the shocking and tragic tale of children at work. The neatly typed pages were bound in a leather folder that Lillian brought to the Governor of New York State.

"New York is not the only state where children are working in the factories and mills. You know as well as I do that if New York were to pass laws forbidding children to work in the factories, the manufacturers of New York State would not be able to compete with the manufacturers of other states," the Governor explained to Lillian.

"But we can't go from state legislature to state legislature. It just wouldn't work," Lillian complained. "We need one law that will apply to all states."

"Broken spirits, untrained hands, and disabled bodies, these are the profits of child labor." Lillian spoke to thousands in meeting halls and colleges around the country. Jane Addams, who founded the first American Settlement House, Hull House in Chicago, joined Lillian

88

and Florence. They founded the National Committee on Child Labor.

They gathered signatures on petitions, they spoke to Congressmen and Senators, womens' clubs, school authorities from East to West and North to South.

Judges, teachers, nurses, housewives and other interested citizens joined the Committee, but the indefatigable little group was no match for the powerful manufacturers who wanted no interference from either the state or the federal government.

"Sometimes I think these people are not human. Greed can do terrible things." Florence was indignant. "What greater riches can a country boast of than healthy and educated children?"

"I know," agreed Lillian, who was more tolerant than Florence of human weakness. "But we won't give up until we get the laws we want."

The State of New York passed a law that made it compulsory for children to attend school until they reached the age of sixteen.

Lillian rejoiced. "We have to measure the small victories too. At least now, we have some government support."

Compulsory schooling is a big victory," Florence admitted. "But I'm still worried about those who are in the factories."

Lillian nodded her head. She was worried, too. I'm more than a little scared. The East Side is full of old wooden factory buildings that employ hundreds of young girls. There are no standards of safety, not to speak of long hours and small wages."

Many of the girls who worked in the factories and lofts of the East Side were members of the Settlement House Social Club. Lillian had often spoken to them about the conditions in the factories.

"I'm really terrified that it's going to take a tragedy before anything is done about those firetraps." Lillian shuddered, thinking of what one of the girls had told her.

"We are actually locked inside. The boss is afraid that the girls are going to steal the clothing they make. The doors are bolted." The girl shivered. "I'm so afraid up there. What will we do if there is a fire? There is no way we can get out." The girl appealed to Lillian. She wanted to get the girls to join a trade union, so they could petition the boss for better working conditions.

"I think a trade union is a wonderful idea." Lillian went to the library to learn all she could about the trade unions.

"A trade union is the only way they can improve themselves," Lillian said, convinced by what she had seen. She became outspoken in encouraging the girls to join the new labor movement that had begun to grow on the East Side.

The wealthy men and women from uptown who had been giving financial support to the Settlement House were sharply critical of Lillian's new labor efforts. They threatened to stop their contributions.

"If Miss Wald is encouraging Socialism, the Settlement House will become a center for radicals," they said.

Jacob Schiff was genuinely disturbed. He had seen

Lillian through all her crusades, and this time he felt that she was playing with fire.

"People have a right to be heard, and these girls have the right to protect themselves against unscrupulous bosses. Their very lives are in danger. Calling them radicals because they want to better themselves is cruel injustice," said Lillian, who refused to become intimidated.

"But the Settlement House and the nurses will lose friends," persisted Mr. Schiff. He was too honest not to tell Lillian the truth as he saw it.

"Then those funds will have to be collected another way. These people simply cannot dictate to me what I can and cannot do. I do not need conditional contributions; they cannot really be friends of the Settlement House if they feel this way. They are interested only in their own reputations.

Lillian was angry and when Mr. Schiff looked at her, he knew he had said enough. Her eyes flashed and her cheeks were a deep pink. Jacob Schiff had been a friend of Lillian's for a long time, and he had never known her to be persuaded by threats. Her faith in the rightness of what she believed in was too great for her feelings to be influenced or changed because someone was calling them uncomplimentary names.

Lillian gave the girls a room in the Settlement House where they could hold their meetings. And she encouraged them to join the union, although too many of them were afraid. The bosses were firing girls who joined the union, and they feared losing their jobs. In too many cases, they were the sole support of their families, and they all had young brothers and sisters. The infant union did not have a chance.

Lillian first knew that something was wrong when she heard the screech of the sirens. Out in the street, people were running. The sky was filling with thick black smoke, and fear-filled screams could be heard for blocks. The nurses grabbed their bags and ran. But it was too late.

The Triangle Shirtwaist Factory was on fire. Bright scarlet ribbons of flame circled the building, and black smoke poured out of the windows. Broken bodies lay scattered on the sidewalk. One hundred and forty-three girls lost their lives jumping out of windows or died trapped inside the burning building. A great crack was made in the sidewalk by the falling bodies of panic-stricken girls.

It took hours for the fire to be brought under control. Long after the flames, the smoke, and the broken bodies had disappeared, the image remained as a burning scar on the conscience of a city.

Lillian comforted a hysterical girl who had witnessed the tragedy. "I still hear them screaming," she cried. "They were like animals trapped in a burning cage." The girl was a capmaker who worked in a factory across the street from the Triangle Shirtwaist Company. She had seen it all from the window.

Tears slid from Lillian's eyes. She had known many of the dead girls. "They were so young, their lives had scarcely begun. They didn't have a chance."

The whole city was shaken by the tragedy. And a giant protest meeting was called at the Metropolitan Opera House.

The Opera House was filled to capacity. A young girl in a drab brown dress quietly and solemnly gave an eye-witness report of the fire. Hidden in her quiet words was the anguish and the cry, "How could human life have been held so cheaply, been so ruthlessly destroyed?"

Florence Kelley clenched her fist. "We should see some action now," she said.

"Yes," said Lillian in a whisper. "And we are going to."

8. The Children's Bureau

Sunlight filtered through the crisp white curtains and filled the dining room with the light of a glorious morning. A sparrow perched on the window sill as if to greet the two women hastily finishing their breakfast.

"We have opened a Pandora's box of troubles, and there is no magic to close it again," Florence sighed. "There is just no end to investigating, and we certainly don't seem to be getting anywhere."

Florence and Lillian had been working almost four years in their crusade for working children. And not one of their recommended laws had been passed.

Lillian had been reading a letter that had come in the morning's mail. Waving the long white envelope like a banner of victory, she said excitedly: "But we are accomplishing something after all. We've just received an invitation to the White House. The President has called a Conference on the Care of Dependent Children. We are to be delegates from New York State."

"You see, there are always people working for you and with you even when you aren't aware of them." For once, Lillian had been able to show Florence that her faith in the President was justified.

"Good," said Florence, getting caught up in Lillian's enthusiasm. "It certainly is about time. But the Children's Bureau is still wrapped up in yards of red tape. And it was never more urgent than it is right now."

"I agree, and I plan to propose it to the President's Conference," Lillian said, remembering everything that had happened on the day she had first proposed a Federal Children's Bureau to President Theodore Roosevelt almost four years earlier.

It had been a crisp winter morning very like this one. Florence had been sitting alone at the breakfast table, reading the newspaper. Lillian, in another room, heard her shout.

Lillian came into the dining room to find Florence furiously pacing the floor. "Listen to this," she had shouted. "The Secretary of Agriculture is going down South to investigate the damage the boll weevil is doing to the cotton crop. The government has time for cotton, but no time for children."

"What a grand idea," Lillian had blurted. "That's what we need, a Bureau to protect children just like the Department of Agriculture protects farmers and crops."

"Splendid," Florance had cried, flashing one of her

radiant smiles. It was odd how often she and Lillian got the same idea almost at the same time. This time it was Lillian who had put the idea into words.

"Who in the government will listen to our plan?" Lillian's face clouded in thought.

"Why not go straight to the President," Florence suggested. And before Lillian could say another word, Florence was on the telephone with her friend, Professor Devine of Columbia University, who knew Theodore Roosevelt well.

Scarcely twenty-four hours later, Lillian Wald was in a private conference with the President of the United States.

"There is a great need for a government agency to protect the children just like the forests, the water supply, the hogs and the lobsters are protected. What more valuable resource does any country have than its children?" Lillian spoke nervously, hoping that she did not sound as if she were lecturing.

President Roosevelt listened carefully and he encouraged her to give him more information.

Lillian explained how the work of the Child Labor Committee had been complicated by having to convince each State Legislature to regulate and supervise children at work. But if a federal agency existed the regulations could be standardized.

"Children need more than laws," Lillian pleaded for the thousands of children in the factories and mills. Investigations into factory conditions can only be properly carried out by an agency of the federal government.

Had she made the President aware of how urgent the

need was? Lillian wondered. The President had listened very carefully, and he had even taken notes.

"I agree wholeheartedly," the President had said. "All I ask is patience. You have given me a big job, which is more easily promised than done."

Lillian's hopes had been raised sky high by the President's reassuring words.

Florence was more skeptical, and each year that passed seemed to prove that she was more realistic than the optimistic Lillian.

Theodore Roosevelt had not even advocated the Children's Bureau to Congress. Florence warned that unless something were done, the Children's Bureau Bill would be forgotten.

When the President called another White House Conference for the Conservation of Natural Resources, Florence filled the room with the electricity of her fury.

"The President seems to have forgotten he made a promise," she said bitterly.

Lillian tried to keep her faith in the face of disappointment. Besides, she was not given to the peaks and valleys of feeling that propelled Florence from one battle to another. Perhaps her years in nursing had given her the patience to sustain faith even in the darkest moments.

Now that the President had called a White House Conference devoted to children, Lillian rejoiced. Her faith no longer seemed so badly misplaced.

The White House Conference was a giant step in the right direction. Of that Lillian was positive.

"You wait and see," she told Florence. The numbers of people who feel as we do are growing."

Lillian went to the first White House Conference on Children with a heart full of hope. Sitting in the large room, Lillian watched the other delegates enter and take their places. The room buzzed with anticipation; this was the first nationwide assembly of child welfare workers, the pioneers of a new profession.

Gradually, the Conference room was filled with two hundred people from all parts of the United States. There were directors of reform schools and orphan homes; there were teachers, judges, nurses, and people whose job it was to take care of orphans in rural counties. They came from small towns and large cities, but they all had one thing in common: they all knew the sadness of the forgotten child, the fear and bitterness of children who are "all alone."

Delegate after delegate told of his own experiences.

"We have only to visit the new juvenile courts to know the unhappy fate that awaits the unloved and neglected child," said a judge from Chicago.

"The new science of psychology is demonstrating how the mind and emotions of the growing child are damaged by neglect," said a professor from a large university.

Protection of children started with keeping families together, Lillian thought to herself. Death or illness, or the want of a few dollars, should not be responsible for the shattering of family ties. In her travels across the country, Lillian had seen small children living in asylums with the derelict and insane. Many small factory workers were recruited from the ugly shacks and dilapidated barns that served as "Poorhouses."

"I go to sleep at night with the image of those little pale and pinched faces looking at the world with eyes full of fear and loneliness," Lillian had once confessed.

When the Conference unanimously approved placing orphaned and abandoned children in the care of foster families instead of in institutions, Lillian almost shouted "Hurray." Foster care for orphans had long been one of her great concerns. The Henry Street nurses had been one of the first agencies to place babies whose mothers could not take care of them in foster homes.

The delegates also agreed to keep destitute families together by giving them government relief.

The appeal of silent children was being heard at last, but how would the Conference be able to carry out its own recommendations? If anything, the Conference had only sharpened the need for a Federal Children's Bureau.

Lillian rose to address the Conference. "The children of the poor, more than all others, need to be prepared for the responsibilities of life that so soon come upon them," Lillian began.

"They, too, have the right to grow up strong and healthy, in mind, body and spirit. I propose the immediate establishment of a Federal Children's Bureau which will supervise the carrying out of our recommendations."

Unanimously, the delegates to the Conference recommended the enactment of the bill to provide for the Children's Bureau.

In two days, people whose only common cause was the welfare of children had found agreement and common purposes. The first White House Conference on Dependent Children became a landmark in the progress of the Child Welfare movement.

Some cities and states began to adopt plans to aid destitute families, and foster family care programs became more widespread. But the Children's Bureau still remained only a shining vision in the minds of its advocates.

"We've come no closer to getting the Children's Bureau then we were seven years ago," Florence sighed.

"The harder we fight, the more we have to fight against. We are just no match for the textile manufacturers. They want no government interference of any kind. But we can't give up." Lillian had heard the arguments of the textile manufacturers many times in Congressional committee hearings.

President Roosevelt had not been able to push the Children's Bureau Bill through Congress. For seven years, Lillian, Florence and their many ardent co-workers continued to work for the establishment of the Bureau. There wasn't the slightest sign of encouragement, but they did not give up. Finally, at the end of President Taft's Administration in 1912, Congress created the Children's Bureau. President William Howard Taft appointed Julia Lathrop from Hull House its first chief.

The Bureau began as a very small agency. Its only staff members were Julia Lathrop and Grace Abbott. Nevertheless, it now existed at last; it was a beginning.

Both Julia Lathrop and Grace Abbott had spent many years working with children in the slums of Chicago. They knew what needed to be done.

The rate of infant deaths all over the country was alarming. But it was impossible to obtain accurate statistics, when many states and counties kept no records of births and deaths.

As one of its first major tasks, the Children's Bureau asked women's clubs all over the country to gather the statistics in their own communities. Willing women cooperated and sent in their reports to the Children's Bureau.

The statistics clearly showed what the Bureau had surmised: there were many more infant deaths among the poor.

"The terrifying thing is that most of these infant deaths can be easily prevented," said Lillian, who had come to Washington to help her friends Julia Lathrop and Grace Abbott.

Lillian agreed to help prepare a series of publications to be put out by the Children's Bureau to teach people the importance of hygiene and pasteurized milk. These publications were sent free of charge to women all over the nation.

Julia Lathrop investigated ways of making milk and drinking water safe for the public, and the Children's Bureau cooperated with local communities across the country to improve their systems of sanitation and keep their water supplies pure.

With its limited funds and staff of two devoted social workers, the Children's Bureau publicized the urgent needs for mothers' pensions, minimum wage laws, and the regulation of child labor. Forty states soon adopted uniform child labor laws, thanks to the vigilance of one small agency in Washington.

The Children's Bureau was living up to Lillian's expectations. It had managed to stimulate interest and activity in every area of child life: health, working conditions, and juvenile delinquency. But Lillian always looked a little further ahead. Her eye was on the next goal, the better one that always seemed to lay ahead.

The Children's Bureau was but one step along the way. Now Lillian dreamed of an enlarged Bureau.

"A Children's Bureau that will bring parents and teachers from all corners of the land. It would be a place where people could see the finest and best-equipped playgrounds, wonderfully spacious kindergartens, children's clubs, and recreation centers." Lillian described her ambitions to Julia Lathrop. "And all of this would be housed in a magnificent building dedicated to America's children." Lillian thought of the beautiful frieze of del Fuggia in Rome, with its beautiful angel children carved in stone.

"The frieze around the Children's Bureau building would show children at play, smiling and free, safe in a land dedicated to their protection." This was a plan for the future; it was something to work for.

9. War!

Lillian had been writing a report at her desk, when she heard the news. One of the boys burst into the room, shouting, "War, there's a war." He showed Lillian the newspaper.

"WAR," screamed the headline in big black letters.

"Europe IS AT WAR."

It was August, 1914, and across the sea the Archduke Francis Ferdinand, heir to the throne of Austria-Hungary, had been shot by a young Serbian. The murder of the Archduke catapulted Europe into World War I.

Shocked and dazed by the declaration of the war that was already raging in Europe, Lillian tried to settle her thoughts. War was against everything Lillian had ever believed. She despised it with every fiber of her being.

As a nurse, Lillian had dedicated herself to saving human life. War meant its destruction.

Restless, Lillian found it impossible to continue writing her report. From her window, she watched the setting sun wrap a layer of spun gold around the tall tower of the Woolworth building.

"There is beauty in these old streets," Lillian thought. The world could learn a great deal from this neighborhood, where so many people of different nationalities have learned to live together in peace."

At that moment, Lillian knew what her role was to be. War never solved any problems. If anything, it intensified conflicts. Dedicated to the prevention of human life, Lillian would do all in her power to keep America from war.

Lillian was not alone in her beliefs. Jane Addams, the Reverend John Haynes Holmes of New York's famous Community Church, Rabbi Stephen S. Wise, and many others joined her in the organization they called the American Union Against Militarism. Lillian was elected president.

Lillian spoke at a large public meeting. "Ever since I have grown to maturity" she said, "I have dedicated my life, all that I am and all that I have to the preservation of life, the promotion of happiness, and the development of good will among people. It would follow as the day follows the night that I could not be a militarist in any sense of that word."

In response to its stirring appeals, the American Union grew from fifteen members to six thousand in its first year.

But the tide of public opinion was rising in favor of America's entry into the war. The peace organization became the target of accusations.

Epithets such as "unpatriotic" and "anti-American" were hurled at Lillian and the other pacifists. Lillian was even accused of being a traitor.

"Let them call me names, I'll stand by my beliefs. War. is tragic, animal, ugly. . . . I will never accept it as inevitable," Lillian retorted.

The peace group was engaged in a constant round of activities—large and small public meetings, lectures, and discussions. The hectic pace taxed Lillian's strength, and she often felt tired and drained. "I know what I have to do. Every minute of speaking and writing will be worth it, if we can keep this country out of war." On a hot summer day, Lillian led a parade of twelve hundred women down the streets of New York.

On one of Lillian's trips to Washington, President Woodrow Wilson shook hands with her warmly. "You know, Miss Wald, how enormous my respect is for you and your work," he said. "I want you to know that, with some reservations, I share your point of view." Lillian was heartened by the policy Wilson tried to follow.

In Congress, the American Union had two staunch friends and advocates for peace, Senators La Follette and Norris. Lillian herself made an eloquent plea for peace before the Senate Committee on Military Affairs.

"If we send arms to the countries at war, our ships will be attacked and then we will be forced to defend them. This can only mean that we will be drawn into the war," Lillian had pleaded.

But the *Lusitania,* a British passenger ship, was destroyed by the Germans. American neutrals had been on board this ship. The nation was thrown into a fever of anti-German feeling. More and more Americans were arguing for America's entry into the war. Passion and militant feeling mounted across the country. "The Germans are America's enemy. We must not forget that the Allies are our friends. Do we not owe something to the democracies across the sea?" people were asking.

President Wilson declared a state of armed neutrality. The American Union Against Militarism warned, "If our ships are armed they will invite attack." But the protests were not heeded, and Congress gave American shipmasters permission to arm their vessels.

"We are asking for trouble. Before you know it, we will be at war," Lillian said sadly, but she continued to speak against war at public meetings.

During those hectic months in 1917, the little American Union Against Militarism was more active than ever. Jane Addams started her own peace committee in Chicago, a committee which became the International League for Peace and Freedom.

In New York, the small group of dedicated pacifists, Lillian Wald, Reverend Holmes, Rabbi Stephen S. Wise, Max Eastman, the noted writer, and Oswald Villard, publisher of the *New York Post,* met every day in a little restaurant on the East Side to plan their strategy. They worked feverishly.

In Europe, the German army was claiming victory in battle after battle. France and Britain were seized by panic, and they looked to America for help.

Lillian, too, condemned the tactics and aggression of the Germans. She was heartily opposed to all that the Germans, the Austro-Hungarians, and the Turks, were fighting for. But above all, Lillian was opposed to war.

The United States declared war on Germany in April, 1917, "to make the world safe for democracy," President Wilson said.

The declaration of war had come so quickly, that for days afterward, Lillian was overcome by shock and grief. It was difficult for her to shake off the sense of despair which seemed to wrap itself around her like a shroud.

Vicious rumors circulated about the neighborhood. Lillian was accused of all kinds of subversive activities— from a spy for the Germans to a saboteur, from a traitor to a coward.

"There are still many people who agree with you," Florence said, trying to rouse Lillian from her melancholy. "It's always the ones who oppose you who make the loudest noises."

"Keep the Settlement House active, and you'll have the best insurance against the hotheads of the neighborhood," encouraged Florence, who felt furious at the unjust accusations.

Lillian had put her reputation at stake, and she felt as if she had lost the biggest battle of her life.

"I simply stood by my convictions," Lillian protested. "I would still stand by them. War is against everything that is decent and I shall always be opposed to it."

What hurt Lillian most was not the name calling, but

the withdrawal of support from both the Settlement House and the Visiting Nurses Service.

"Let them call me names, but why do they have to hurt the Nurses' Service?" Lillian asked. She was deeply worried about the lack of funds and the future of the Service. "This is the torture chamber method of punishment," she cried.

People who had called themselves her friends no longer wanted to be associated with Lillian Wald. Among them were many wealthy philanthropists whose donations had made it possible to carry on the work of the Settlement House.

"Is the work of my entire life going to suffer because I dared to speak for peace? Our nurses are going to care for the families of the soldiers no less than the other sick." Lillian's old determination returned. She had no intention of seeing her life's work destroyed.

The Nurses' Service needed her now more than ever. Bracing herself, Lillian decided to attempt to ignore the rumors and gossip. She declared, "If I need comfort I'll take it from my work. There's a big job to do."

"You needn't look so grim," Florence teased. "I knew you'd come around. You're too much the born optimist for anything to keep your spirits down for very long."

Lillian found new strength in knowing that she was still needed. Somehow, she felt sustained during those dark and defeated days.

"War is like a disease; it has to run its course before it is spent. All we can do now is treat its worst symptoms and for this, we need good nurses." Lillian urged President Wilson to give nurses rank and authority in the Army.

The United States Army established its own School of Nursing. When Lillian was asked for advice concerning the setting up of a new school, she recommended that Annie Goodrich be appointed its Director. Her suggestion was acted on, and Annie Goodrich left the Visiting Nurses Service to become head of the first Army School of Nursing.

"My own work is here among my neighbors," Lillian announced, making the Settlement her base of operations.

Under Lillian's direction, the Settlement House played a large part in the war effort. Located in the midst of the teaming tenement district, the Settlement was a logical center for the distribution of information and propaganda.

Several of the offices were moved to make space for the headquarters of the Food Council, the Red Cross, and the new Baby Saving Campaign.

The Settlement House now occupied three buildings, and an entire building was given over to the draft board. A resident of the Settlement House assumed charge of the board so that neighborhood boys were introduced to the Army by a friendly and familiar person.

Children always suffered the most in times of war. Families were separated, and homes were broken when fathers became soldiers. Lillian expanded the social clubs and added more classes to the Settlement House, offering larger numbers of children wholesome recreation and an opportunity to take their minds off their loneliness.

The war bled the nation, and the world. Thousands of young men died on the battlefields. And as if that were not enough, the war sent a scourge whipping around the world.

Spanish Influenza hit New York with the force of a tornado in the fall of 1918. Within four days, five hundred cases of pneumonia and influenza were reported to the Henry Street nurses.

Panic seized the city. The Red Cross set up the Nurses Emergency Council. Lillian Wald was asked to be Chairman.

The war had created a grave shortage of doctors, nurses, hospitals, medical supplies—and even gravediggers and shroudmakers. There were not enough trained personnel to answer the city's call for help.

Lillian used every resource at her command; she reorganized her entire nursing staff to meet the emergency. Nurses were sent out in shifts, day and night.

"There's a desperate shortage of nurses. We will have to recruit volunteers on the street to relieve the nurses of every other duty." The public health nurses were needed as never before.

Lillian ordered handbills to be printed asking for volunteers to work with the nurses in homes and hospitals. The printshop around the corner from the Settlement ran its presses all night so that the handbills would be ready for distribution the next morning.

"We have turned the city into a gigantic field hospital," Lillian announced, too numb to feel her exhaustion.

Every single medical, health, and social service

agency was called upon to help. Housewives, businessmen, bankers, the Salvation Army, society ladies, college
students and factory workers worked side by side—in
the laundries, the kitchens, and the wards of the city's
hospitals.

For one solid month, the Nurses' Emergency Council
worked to bring the wild epidemic under control.

"If anything, this experience should teach us how
great is the need for trained nurses in the community."
Lillian thanked everyone who had taken part in the
splendid mobilization.

But in her report to the Red Cross, Lillian also called
attention to the tragic failures caused by untrained
people who had panicked, bungled, or even abandoned
their jobs. "A little foresight would have prevented so
much loss of life," she declared.

"We were ready for a war three thousand miles away,
but totally unprepared and disarmed for a battle right in
our own backyard," Lillian said, warning against com-
placency toward the problems which still persisted at
home.

The recognition of the public health nurse had been
won, but there was still a long way to go before the full
extent of her contribution would be realized.

On the battlefield, the American Army brought new
hope and strength. In bloody combat, the Germans were
challenged and defeated, and the stalemate was broken.
With a great shout, the Allies announced their "victory."
And the victorious armies turned homeward to the rous-
ing welcome of their homelands.

Lillian felt a curious mixture of emotion as she watched

the soldiers returning. Her heart was glad for the boys and men who returned whole and healthy; and heavy with sorrow for the broken in body and spirit.

"Now is the time to guarantee the peace and build a ring of friendship around the world, so that war will be forever banished," Lillian said at the celebration at the Settlement House that evening.

There were crepe paper streamers and balloons, there were speeches and songs—and there was hope for a better world to come.

10. *Cannes 1919*

The waves, rippled gold by the sunlight, swirled around the ocean liner that was carrying the American delegates to the first international conference on Public Health. Lillian Wald, Dr. William Welch, Dr. Emmet Holt and Dr. Herman Biggs were on their way to the beautiful city of Cannes, France, where the International Red Cross had called the Conference.

All during the war, Lillian had worked and planned for an international conference on Public Health. It had been her hope and her dream.

"Public Health is a concern of all mankind and the public health nurse is a link in the chain of friendship that will someday circle the world," Lillian had said at the first meeting of the National Organization of Public

Health Nurses, the first professional association of public health workers. Once the organization was formed, they had honored the tireless leader by unanimously choosing Lillian Wald to be its first president.

In her address as president, Lillian had declared, "We have barely begun. The whole world is waiting for us."

Now, standing on the ship's deck, Lillian watched the waves foam as they hit the sides of the ship.

"It has taken me twenty-five years to take this journey," she mused, remembering her first steps with Mary Brewster on the streets of the lower East Side.

The journey had been far from smooth, but Public Health Nursing had come a long long way from its early days on Henry Street.

How could Lillian ever forget Dr. Wheeler, who would not permit her to take sick babies out of the hospital and to put them in foster homes, where they could be cared for by Lillian's nurses. It had been so cruel to leave those babies in sterile hospital corridors, where they pined away from sheer loneliness.

Lillian had come to Dr. Wheeler with her foster home plan, and the doctor had refused to cooperate. "It is too great a responsibility, Miss Wald." We can only give these babies the care they need in a hospital," Dr. Wheeler had said.

"Posh," Lillian had said. She was going to prove the rightness of her plan to the doctor. She told her nurses: "Every baby we know whose mother is unable to care for it is to be placed in a foster home. I have a list of carefully chosen homes, where women are eager and able to care for these children."

Lillian herself had been astounded by the success of her "Boarding Out" plan. Even now she could not help but feel a little surge of pride that it had turned out so well. Four times as many babies had died in hospitals as under the care of Lillian's nurses in the foster homes. Dr. Wheeler had to swallow her pride and agree that Lillian was right.

It always seemed that when one battle was won, there were others waiting.

East Side women used midwives to deliver their babies, just as their mothers had done. No one thought it was important to have a doctor.

Hundreds of mothers and babies died in childbirth. Lillian had felt that most of those deaths could be avoided if the babies were delivered with strict regard for antiseptic cleanliness. She recalled that first class for midwives at the Henry Street Settlement. Most of the women had seemed angry and resentful. They had been midwives for many years, and this had been the first time that anyone had questioned their methods. Lillian had been so careful not to appear doubtful or critical of their abilities. She had treated them like fellow nurses.

"What is there for me to learn?" one old woman had asked. "About babies, I know," she had said tartly.

"I am interested in your methods. A midwife is very much like a nurse," Lillian had said reassuringly.

"You have all had times when the delivery did not turn out well, and infection and sickness came to the mother and the baby. Your methods are good, but I would like to show you how you can prevent infection. And I am sure that there is much you can teach me."

At this the women had nodded their heads, and their angry expressions had softened into smiles. The nurse had said that she approved of their methods. Well, they would show her that they were not too old to learn. After all, wasn't a midwife's reputation built on how many of her babies were born alive?

The first school for midwives had been successfully established on the East Side.

It had been easier getting nurses into the factories than into the schools. Thank goodness for the willingness of Dr. Lederle, Lillian thought, remembering those difficult days when so many children were kept out of school needlessly, while others attended school with highly contagious illnesses.

Lillian had persuaded the Metropolitan Life Insurance Company to provide trained nurses to care for injured factory workers.

"Wouldn't it be to your advantage to see that injured workers are getting the proper care? Think how many people could be saved from permanent injury by immediate treatment," she had told the official of the Life Insurance Company. And the man had been wise enough to test Lillian's plan. Large factories bought large policies from the Metropolitan Life Insurance Company to protect themselves from lawsuits whenever a worker was injured on the job. Lillian's plan had saved the Insurance Company thousands of dollars, and at the same time it had prevented needless tragedies. The plan had been so successful that other insurance companies

wasted no time in employing trained nurses. The insurance companies also began to print booklets advising people how to protect themselves from sickness, accident and injury.

"There is no end to the work of a nurse in her community." Lillian felt a quiet pride welling up in her. The Henry Street Nurses had served more than thirty-thousand people in New York City.

Public Health Nursing as a profession had grown with the expanding vision of its pioneer nurse. Lillian felt deeply about the calling of the nurse. She was part of a great movement dedicated to enhance and preserve human life.

"Our work has barely begun," she murmured again. "The whole world is waiting for us."

Great Britain, France, Italy, Japan and the United States had sent delegates to the conference called by the Red Cross Societies of the world. In Cannes, a new war was declared—a war against disease and a war that would unite the world.

Lillian was on the Committee of Nurses. It did not take very long for a plan very similar to that which Lillian Wald and Mary Brewster had put into action on the streets of New York to be developed.

In addition to the plan for public health nurses to visit people in their homes, a new plan was established for the training of women interested in becoming nurses from countries that had no schools of nursing. Lillian proposed the establishment of a world center for the training of nurses in the field of public health.

"We have only to look about us here in France to see the benefits of such a program," Lillian said, thinking of the hundreds of homeless children roaming about the French countryside in search of what had once been their homes.

What was to become of these children who had been orphaned by the war? The Americans had helped set up temporary shelters for these children, but there was a severe shortage of French nurses to staff the homes which were being established as permanent asylums.

The children were the most tragic reminders of the war that had raged but a few months before. The battle-fields were marked by the deathly still, lonely graves. The scars of war were written in the faces of the children as well as in the ruins of villages, towns and cities.

"The way to build a lasting peace is through the kind of international cooperation that this conference represents," Lillian declared.

"Some day people will know how much more there is to be gained by bringing us together in friendship than by separating us in hatred."

The conference had accomplished its goals. Plans of mutual help had been formed. Even as the conference concluded, Lillian was invited to Paris to help France train her nurses in Public Health.

In Paris, Lillian arranged for French nurses to take their training at the Henry Street Settlement under the auspices of the Visiting Nurses Service.

Lillian returned to the United States to find that her mother seemed to have aged in her absence, and was ailing. Minnie Wald was an old lady now, and Lillian was concerned about her mother's health.

"Mother needs to be away from the hustle and bustle of the Settlement," Lillian had written to her sister Julia. Lillian purchased a rambling house in the country, where her mother could rest away from the excitement of Henry Street. The House On The Pond, as Lillian named the country retreat, was an ideal hideaway in Westport, Connecticut. Here was a place where her mother could enjoy the serenity of country living and have time just to sit and read her Bible.

Minnie looked forward to the weekends Lillian spent with her, but they were too few and far between. Guilt began to nag Lillian, but try as she would to leave the city, she could not help herself. There was too much keeping her there.

"Mother wants me to do my work," she told herself. "She'd hate the thought of being the one to keep me from it."

Lillian was once again on a whirl of speaking tours. This time she was pleading the cause of the wives and babies of mountaineers and miners, the farmers and workers in the backroads of America.

"More than 150,000 babies under one year of age are dying every year. Many of these are sacrifices to ignorance and lack of medical care." Lillian spoke before the White House Conference on Women and Children. She told the story of an isolated farm woman in Burnt Forks, Wyoming, whose simple tragic tale dramatized the plight of thousands of women in rural communities across the nation.

During a terrible blizzard in Burnt Fork, a young father had gone out to get help for his wife, who was desperately ill. Attracted by a light in a distant cottage, the man fought his way through the blinding flurries of snow. He knocked on the door of the cottage. "Please help me," he cried, "I'm afraid that my wife is dying."

The couple who lived in the cottage rushed back to the dying woman. They got there just in time to take the baby.

The woman had two children of her own, and she was frightened. What could they do, they had so little money? Had she done the right thing to take the baby, or was she depriving her own children? The woman sat up that night grieving for the tiny infant in her arms. A magazine lay open on the table in front of her, and it happened to contain an article written by Lillian Wald. It had something to do with the care of infants, and the woman read it carefully.

When she had finished, she wrote Lillian a letter: "I am writing to you because you seem like 'real folks' and will understand my problem." The woman confided to Lillian her worries and fears for her childrens' health because there was no doctor or nurse nearby on whom she could call. And because she did not have enough milk to give to the baby.

Lillian advised her by mail and arranged to have milk sent to her. And when she checked on the medical services available to the woman, she discovered that the nearest nursing service was sixty miles away in Salt Lake City, Utah.

The appeal of that farm woman in Burnt Fork set the wheels in motion as Lillian told her story at the White

House Conference. The Conference recommended that Congress share the expense of medical care in outlying districts with individual states.

Congress appropriated the money that made it possible for the Town and Country service of the Red Cross to reach those who lived far from the cities and larger towns. Red Cross nurses often had to travel on horseback, but thousands of women began to receive aid and instruction in the care of themselves and their babies. The number of deaths of infants and mothers began to decline.

At Henry Street, Lillian had arranged the nurses' schedule in three shifts, so that there were always nurses to answer maternity and other emergency calls, no matter what time of day or night they came in.

The city was still plagued by great health problems. The tidal wave of immigration from across the sea had ended with the war; but the growth of the new industries attracted thousands of newcomers to the cities. The worst of the tenements were gone, and the grimy gray wooden factory buildings had been demolished. Suicide Hall, the saloons, and the most disreputable of the pool halls were also gone. But there was still terrible overcrowding, unemployment, and undernourishment.

"The aim of any public health program is disease prevention. In the early days our only weapon against contagion was the isolation of the sick. But new discoveries have given us new and more effective weapons. Diphtheria can now be prevented by innoculation." Lillian searched for a plan that would permit all the children in the city to be innoculated against the dreaded child killer.

"What good are all the new medical discoveries if there is no way for people to benefit from them?" Lillian asked. She began to argue for the establishment of health centers all over the city. "If we were to apply all our new medical knowledge, we could not only prevent smallpox and diphtheria from becoming epidemics, but we could also spot tuberculosis early enough to spare the heartbreak of family separations."

Lillian planned the East Harlem demonstration center carefully. It was staffed by Henry Street nurses and supported by Henry Street funds.

The health center proved itself within one year. Hundreds of children were innoculated against diphtheria, and hundreds of adults were given chest X-rays for the first time. And people who showed evidence of tuberculosis were treated before the disease became disabling.

The Department of Health of New York City took over the three health centers that Lillian had begun, and made them the backbone of a city-wide health program.

Minnie Wald passed away in December of 1923. Lillian was overcome by grief. "If only I could have spent more time with her," she brooded. Lillian tortured herself with guilt, and buried her guilt in more and more work. Jacob Schiff died in the same year, and Lillian deeply mourned the passing of one of her dearest friends.

"It will be so hard to realize that he isn't here anymore," Lillian told Lavinia. "He was always here when we needed him."

Lillian buried her sorrows the only way she knew

how. She drew her strength from knowing that there were still those who needed her.

Lillian worked herself almost beyond human limits. She never bothered to wait for an elevator; it took less time to run up the steps. Papers and books wanting her attention were always stacked at her bedside table, where she could work on them late at night or in the early morning hours. Visitors to the Settlement were always greeted by Lillian herself. She could never wait for people to come to her.

At fifty-three Lillian was tired, so tired that she felt weak. Every ounce of her old energy seemed to have been drained from her body. New lines of weariness carved themselves into her face. Bad colds frequently made her their victim. But Lillian tried to ignore the aches and pains. She refused to take it easy; she couldn't.

Lillian was late and she was rushing to get dressed. Suddenly a searing pain pierced her chest. For a full minute, she struggled to get her breath before she plunged into thick black darkness.

Lavinia heard the strange gasping, and she rushed into Lillian's room. When there was no answer to her frantic knocking, Docky pushed the door open. She found Lillian unconscious on the floor. She screamed for help.

Now Lillian would have to rest. She had no choice. After a few weeks in the hospital, Lillian was forced to spend her days quietly at the House On The Pond.

At first the country house and country living were a joy. The country home was a good place to recover her strength. But as the weeks stretched into months, Lillian began to feel as if she were in jail.

"I am ashamed of my weakness and not a little annoyed at myself," Lillian confessed to her friends.

When visitors came, Lillian pumped them for news. She insisted that she be kept informed of everything that was happening at the Settlement.

Idleness gnawed at her and gave her no peace.

"Why don't you spend this time writing your biography?" Lavinia suggested.

"No biography is true. It only tells one side of the story," Lillian retorted, annoyed at the suggestion. But she did settle down to write some magazine articles.

Lillian needed rest; only rest could make her well again. And it was taking too long for her strength to return. The spring, summer, and fall of 1925 were long, slow months of convalescence.

From her chair in the garden near the pond, Lillian watched the changing of the seasons. She wasted little time thinking about the past. Her thoughts were all with the Settlement and plans for the future.

"But what if I never have the strength to go back?" The gloomy thought nagged at her constantly, and made it difficult for her to take the rest she was supposed to have.

"I will come back, I have to," she said over and over again to herself. But she had to prove to herself that she was going to be able to come back. By the time November came around, Lillian could stand it no longer. She returned to the Settlement House.

It was hard for her to know what her limits were. "I

do not know that I have done too much until after it is done, for I feel like doing a million things more than I can do," Lillian complained to Lavinia.

Docky tried to insist that she spend time away from the busy Settlement, before the press of work clamped her into her old routine. But Lillian protested, "I have been away long enough."

A fall down a full flight of stairs put Lillian back to bed. And she realized that she had come back too soon.

Her sister Julia came to Henry Street and insisted that Lillian go with her to Florida. "That will be far enough to keep you from rushing back the minute you begin to feel better."

Lillian was forced to admit that a trip to Florida was a good idea, and she consented to go with Julia.

Recuperating in the sunshine, Lillian began to feel her old self. The bright sun and balmy air lifted the gloom that had settled so heavily on her spirits. "I'm almost feeling gay," she wrote to her friends at the Settlement, "because I know now that I am able to come back."

11. *A Promise Fulfilled*

Lillian returned to Henry Street in the spring of 1926. Her spirits were high and she was back at work. "It feels so good to be doing things again," she said, off on her round of meetings and conferences.

The face of the East Side had changed; the grimy old wooden tenements had disappeared, along with the garbage-filled alleys. But the gaunt-eyed face of poverty still haunted the streets, and the number of workingmen without jobs was growing.

The nurses came to Lillian with reports of increasing unemployment. Lillian went to business and government leaders to plead with them to do something to improve the situation before it was too late.

"But Miss Wald, the country is rich. There is prosperity. You have only to read the newspapers to know that," they said.

"I know there is prosperity, but it is floating like cream at the top," Lillian retorted. "Those at the bottom have no share." She knew that the unskilled workers of the East Side had no taste of the riches that the newspapers boasted about.

The papers shouted their optimism about the nation's economy. This was the Roaring Twenties, the era of the flapper, and gay sparkling parties. The automobile had come into its own. Will Rogers, the great comedian, had remarked: "The country might go to the poorhouse, but it would ride there in an automobile."

These were exciting and wonderful years: Charles Lindbergh made his record flight across the Atlantic Ocean. But these were not easy times for the people of the East Side, where it was still a problem to keep hunger at bay. As families who had been successful moved away from the lower East Side into the newer and more fashionable parts of the city, the ghostly spectre of despair became more and more visible.

"Nobody wants to live here anymore," Lillian said sadly. "If only there was decent housing to attract people to the neighborhood."

"People have a right to decent homes. A model housing development would put the tenements to shame." Lillian tried to persuade the Mayor, Jimmy Walker, to build apartment houses. When the Mayor did not act, Herbert Lehman, who was soon to become Governor of New York State, financed a private housing development.

Lillian watched it go up with admiration. "It's the East Side of the future," she said. "Perhaps it will prove to the builders of the city that good housing is a sound business investment."

The Visiting Nurses were getting more and more calls from people who had no money. "My husband has lost his job," was a cry they heard again and again.

Lillian had lived through five depressions on the East Side—and she was only too familiar with the agony of the unemployed, who were always put at the mercy of the charities.

"The saddest thing is to watch the corrosion of family life," Lillian observed. "It always begins with the loss of dignity suffered by men who cannot find work." Lillian urged financial and business leaders to see that there were enough jobs to go around. But they did not pay attention to her warning.

The news flashed like lightning across the nation and around the world, shattering the dreams and hopes of millions. Panic engulfed the nation like an ocean of angry waves.

The stock market crashed in 1929, and the country plunged into the biggest depression in its history. New industries foundered and flopped, old ones closed their doors, and across the nation millions of men were without work.

"Fear has entered the heart of the nation, and it stalks like a black beast," said Lillian. "Nowhere is the situation more tragic than it is among the unskilled and low-paid laborers here on the East Side."

Lillian was in her sixties, and she was fighting a constant battle with her health. Her friends quietly removed the bedside telephone from her room, so that she could sleep undisturbed.

"How odd," remarked Harriet Knight, a Settlement House nurse and close friend of Lillian's, "that she hasn't protested."

"I'm afraid she is relieved," commented one of the younger nurses.

Lillian experienced a feeling of helplessness. The outlook had never seemed so bleak before. The pathetic sight of the long lines of hungry people standing in rain and snow for a cup of hot soup and a slice of bread struck Lillian forcefully.

"Starvation is very real to hundreds of people. And it places them at the mercy of charities, who do nothing more than temporarily hold off starvation." Lillian told the Congressional Committee of the plight of the unemployed on the East Side. "Isn't it the responsibility of the government to uphold the dignity of its citizens?" she asked. Lillian had worked with Fiorello LaGuardia, Frances Perkins and Herbert Lehman to plan a real relief program, one that would be able to provide work instead of charity. She described the plan to the Congressmen.

"There are roads to be built, and dams and canals. Why can't the government hire the unemployed to build these utilities? The entire nation would benefit."

"Relief should not be considered charity. Self-reliance is the root of dignity. And without dignity a human being begins to be destroyed." Lillian pleaded again and again for the formation of a federal agency to provide work for the unemployed.

Day by day, week by week, Lillian saw more and more of her neighbors defeated. Their families fell apart under the burden of despair. "I can't endure the loss of dignity to people who become beggars for a job."

Too often, these unhappy people took out their hurt and their loss of pride on the only ones they could—on the only ones that cared. Angry and resentful, the ones that had cared, cared no longer, and turned away. Security seemed gone for everyone. Children had to live with the knowledge that society had no place for them. Gangs of rebellious boys roamed the neighborhood in search of mischief. They had to fight back against the grownups, who no longer seemed to care about them.

"When the family falls apart, grief and despair and plain hatred rush in to fill the void." Lillian grieved for all the unhappiness she saw around her.

Every day another family found itself homeless. They were evicted, their belongings piled on the street, because they could not pay the rent.

At the foot of Henry Street, a colony of unemployed men made their homes in the tin shacks that were once used as warehouses. The colony was called Tin Mountain. When homeless families had no place to go, they went to Tin Mountain or moved in with another family. Two and three and sometimes four families were forced to live together. Undernourishment and overcrowding caused the tensions to run high. Children tried to find solace in the streets.

"Young people need to know that society does have a

place for them. They must not be allowed to feel cast off and alone." Lillian made it her personal mission to reassure lonely young people.

"Words alone will not do it. And preaching is little more than hypocrisy. We have to show them by making them feel welcome at the Settlement House at all times of the day and night," Lillian said vehemently. "I only wish we had the funds to increase our facilities."

There were no funds, but the art and music classes were still enlarged and the gym was always open. Every Saturday night there was a dance for young people. A small price of ten cents was charged for admission, but for those without the dime, admission was always free.

Disease always follows on the heels of hunger. Calls to the Nursing Service were coming in at a rate no one could have anticipated. Lillian was consumed with worry that the nurses would not have the funds to continue their work.

"The Nurses' Service has its back to the wall, and it is being pushed beyond its limits. The nurses are accomplishing miracles. They are answering calls all over the city." Lillian talked to the Mayor. But Jimmy Walker was busy with other things.

"The budget is bursting at the seams, and people cannot contribute the way they used to," Lillian said, as she began the distasteful job of fund raising. She had never liked to plead for money, but there was no choice. The Settlement was providing free milk as well as supporting twenty health centers.

"We are caring for 75,000 patients," Lillian told people all over the city, "but our work is threatened by a serious lack of funds." Lillian appealed for city support for the Visiting Nurses Service.

"There is so much to do and so little time," Lillian complained. She was working with a sense of urgency as if she knew that time was against her.

Lillian was in Washington one day and New York the next. Across the country, the unemployed were marching, pleading for work, for jobs. A sense of shame and violation echoed from New York to California. When Franklin Delano Roosevelt was elected President of the United States, a new wave of hope swept the nation.

When Roosevelt took office, the depression had reached its lowest point. President Roosevelt put Lillian's plan for relief into a federal program. The Works Projects Administration was the name given to the federal agency whose job it was to provide employment. Only projects of long-range value were considered. Under this program workers built thousands of miles of roads, erected many public buildings, and built or improved hundreds of parks. Slowly, the curtain of darkness lifted as the country began to recover.

"I feel young from the neck up," Lillian remarked one day—but her old weakness had returned, more intense and more draining than before. She had been pushing herself for too long. Her heart was weakened and she began to suffer from a rare type of anemia. She was in and out of the hospital for tests and treatment.

At long last inactivity was forced upon her. Perhaps retirement was to be the greatest test of her spirit she was yet to face.

The House On The Pond was her home now. And Lillian slowly began to face the idea of her retirement from active work. Helen Hall came from a Philadelphia Settlement House to become the head worker of the House on Henry Street. Helen had been a trusted friend.

"I'm grateful it's you who's getting my job," Lillian confided to Helen. "At least I know it's in good hands."

As soon as she felt stronger, Lillian realized that she had to keep herself busy. Idleness made her feel like a slacker—a thought she could scarcely abide. And she set herself to write her second book about the Henry Street Settlement House. *Windows on Henry Street* was published the next year (Lillian wrote her first book about the Henry Street Settlement in 1917. It was titled *The House on Henry Street.*)

Hundreds of letters asking for help and advice were sent to her. Lillian answered each one and referred the writers to agencies which could help them.

On her birthday in March, 1937, Lillian received more messages of congratulations than she could count. President Roosevelt commemorated "The many years you have spent in unselfish labor to promote the happiness and well-being of others."

Mayor Fiorello LaGuardia presented Lillian with the Distinguished Service Certificate of New York City. And an old neighbor wrote: "What you get out of this house" (referring to the Settlement House), "you can't put in your pocket." Lillian got almost as many telegrams from around the world as she did when the fortieth year of Settlement House was celebrated.

At that time, gifts and letters full of glowing tributes had been sent to Lillian too. "I have had love and friendship beyond my desserts," she had said.

Lillian was very happy: "Forty years on the East Side, and I am still alive to see my most cherished dreams come true." Perhaps she could not run around the way she used to, but that did not mean that she could not still savor life.

Lillian's interest in the world around her, in life and people, did not waver for a moment. She kept up her correspondence with friends around the world.

Lillian spent those quiet years surrounded by the beauty of the country. Her neighbors in Westport soon became as close as her neighbors on the East Side. And the sparkling blue pond in front of her house was filled with the laughter of children. Rare was the weekend when the house was not packed with visitors.

"I'm almost beginning to enjoy retirement," Lillian confided to Eleanor Roosevelt, who was then the First Lady of the land. "At last, I'm beginning to catch up on my letters, and to do the writing I never really had time for," Lillian winked at Mrs. Roosevelt. "And to get to really know my friends."

After a short illness, Lillian's eyes closed for the last time in December, 1940.

The death of Lillian Wald was mourned around the world. Thousands of people felt deeply the hurt of losing a very dear and intimate friend.

As Lillian had said of Florence Kelley, "What she had been can never be gone or lost." So it was of Lillian herself. "What she had been would live forever."

The greatness of Lillian Wald needed no monument of stone. Her monuments were all alive, and she had built them herself.

Dr. William Welch had cited the Public Health Nurse as one of America's three greatest contributions to the cause of medical progress.

The Henry Street Settlement is still devoted to its neighbors. It is one of the most famous and active Settlement Houses in the United States today. Children from all parts of the city come to Henry Street for music, art and drama classes. Social workers from all over the world come to study its operation and its facilities. It is in the forefront of the nation's war on juvenile deliquency.

The Henry Street Settlement House is still the "House with a Heart."

New housing developments have changed the face of the lower East Side. One of these low-income housing projects is called the Lillian Wald Houses.

The Nurses' Clinic and its staff has been moved to Bellevue Hospital, where the Visiting Nurse Service continues to function with the same sense of high purpose and public interest it had when it was created.

The Children's Bureau is working close to the vision Lillian cherished. It serves as a clearinghouse and information center for all the research and work done in Child Welfare.

Surely Lillian had the best minds and the most dedicated hands working with her. The list of her friends and co-workers is long and distinguished. But would these fine workers and great leaders have come together in common cause if it were not for the greatness of Lillian Wald? Perhaps that was the nugget of her greatness

—her splendid ability to bring the most diverse personalities together and keep them working in harmony until the goal was reached. But there was more to Lillian Wald.

Lillian Wald was a nurse, a social worker, an administrator. With a heart full of love, a spirit full of courage, and a head full of dreams, Lillian Wald gave something to the world that cannot be taken away.

Lillian Wald, by having lived in the way she chose, made the world a better place for everyone.

Acknowledgments

The author wishes to acknowledge, with gratitude, the co-operation of the staff of the Henry Street Settlement. Mr. Hyman Schroeder, to whom Lillian Wald was a dear friend and whose childhood reminiscence made her vibrant spirit come alive for me. The late Rev. John Haynes Holmes, who shared so many adventures with the heroine of this biography and who advised, "You've got a big fish there, and to catch a big fish you need a big net." And finally, the encouragement and patience of my husband, Robert Rogow, who though often pressed for time, read these pages again and again until they reached their final form.

We are grateful to the Visiting Nurse Service of New York for providing the photograph of Lillian Wald used for the frontispiece.

SALLY ROGOW

Bibliography

BOOKS ABOUT LILLIAN WALD (*Source Books*)

Duffus, R. J., *Lillian Wald, Neighbor and Crusader,* New York, 1938.
Wald, Lillian, *The House On Henry Street,* New York, 1917.
Wald, Lillian, *Windows On Henry Street,* New York, 1930.

BOOKS ABOUT OTHER SETTLEMENT HOUSES

Addams, Jane, *First Twenty Years At Hull House,* New York, 1930.
Addams, Jane, *Second Twenty Years At Hull House, September 1909-September 1929,* New York, 1930.

BOOKS FOR YOUNG PEOPLE

Dodge, Bertha S. *The Story of Nursing,* Boston, 1954.
Williams (Epstein) Beryl, *The Angel of Henry Street,* New York, 1948.

COVENANT BOOKS

Stories of Jewish men and women to inspire and instruct young people

1. SILVERSMITH OF OLD NEW YORK: *Myer Myers*
   by William Wise

2. BORDER HAWK: *August Bondi*
   by Lloyd Alexander

3. THE WORLD OF JO DAVIDSON
   by Lois Harris Kuhn

4. JUBAL AND THE PROPHET
   by Frieda Clark Hyman

5. THE UNCOMMON SOLDIER: *Major Alfred Mordecai*
   by Robert D. Abrahams

6. THE VOICE OF LIBERTY: *Emma Lazarus*
   by Eva Merriam

7. KEYS TO A MAGIC DOOR: *Isaac Leib Peretz*
   by Silvia Rothchild

8. ABOAB, FIRST RABBI OF THE AMERICAS
   by Emily Hahn

9. NORTHWEST PIONEER: *Louis Fleischner*
   by Alfred Apsler

10. ALBERT EINSTEIN: *Citizen of the World*
    by William Wise

11. BUILDERS OF JERUSALEM: *In the Time of Nehemiah*
    by Frieda Clark Hyman

12. FLAGSHIP HOPE: *Aaron Lopez*
    by Lloyd Alexander

13. SCHOLAR-FIGHTER: *Saadia Gaon*
    by L. M. Klapperman

14. SOUND OF BOW BELLS: *Sir David Salomons*
    by Robert D. Abrahams

—